The American
Avant-Garde
Tradition

The American Avant-Garde Tradition

William Carlos Williams,
Postmodern Poetry, and the
Politics of Cultural Memory

John Lowney

Lewisburg
Bucknell University Press
London: Associated University Presses

Associated University Presses
440 Forsgate Drive
Cranbury, NJ 08512

Associated University Presses
16 Barter Street
London WCIA 2AH, England

Associated University Presses
P.O. Box 338, Port Credit
Mississauga, Ontario
Canada L5G 4L8

The paper used in this publication meets the requirements
of the American National Standard for Permanence of Paper
for Printed Library Materials Z39.48-1984

Library of Congress Cataloging-in-Publication-Data

Lowney, John, 1957–
    The American avant-garde tradition : William Carlos Williams,
postmodern poetry, and the politics of cultural memory / John
Lowney.
        p.   cm.
    Includes bibliographical references and index.
    ISBN 0-8387-5333-7 (alk. paper)
    1. Williams, William Carlos, 1883–1963—Criticism and
interpretation. 2. Politics and literature—United States-
-History—20th century. 3. American poetry—20th century—History
and criticism. 4. Experimental poetry, American—History and
criticism. 5. Williams, William Carlos, 1883–1963—Influence.
6. Postmodernism (Literature)—United States. 7. Avant-garde
(Aesthetics)—United States. 8. Influence (Literary, artistic,
etc.) 9. Canon (literature) I. Title.
PS3545.I544Z62   1997
811'.52—dc 20   96-7249
                                                                 CIP
SECOND PRINTING 1998
PRINTED IN THE UNITED STATES OF AMERICA

For Kay Lowney

and in memory of
John T. Lowney (1922–1995)

Contents

Acknowledgments

I am fortunate to have many friends and colleagues who have made the writing of this book a rewarding experience, and I am grateful to the teachers who extended support during the early stages of this project. Mutlu Konuk Blasing provided thoughtful guidance in the formation of this book and has set for me an outstanding example as a scholar and critic of American poetry. Robert Scholes and George Monteiro have each balanced astute criticism with continual encouragement in the project's value. And working with Randy Blasing has made me a better reader of contemporary poetry.

I cannot thank enough the colleagues whose friendship and intellectual companionship since the beginning of this project have made it all worthwhile, especially José Aranda, Randy Bass, Rosemary Marangoly George, Pam Hardman, Yuko Matsukawa, and Mark Sanders, who have read and commented on various parts of the manuscript. Of the many colleagues whose questions and discussion at conferences have furthered this project, I thank particularly Burton Hatlen, whose tireless work on behalf of objectivist poetry is inestimable. The Grinnell College English Department and the Illinois Benedictine College Arts and Humanities Faculty have also given me opportunities to present parts of the manuscript; I am appreciative of the questions raised by both audiences. While at Illinois Benedictine, I have been fortunate to have Jeffrey DeShell and Lisa Sheffield as friends whose advice and sense of humor have always been timely. I am especially grateful for Ashley Cross's presence as a colleague and companion; her wit, warmth, and insight have meant more to me than I could have imagined. Finally, I thank my parents, to whom this book is dedicated, not only for their enthusiastic support but for teaching me to appreciate the pleasures of language.

I am grateful to those people who have worked on this book at Bucknell University Press and Associated University Presses. This book has benefited from the suggestions for revision offered by Mills F. Edgerton Jr. and the anonymous reader for Bucknell University Press. I thank Julien Yoseloff, Evelyn Apgar, and Wyatt Benner at Associated University Presses for their excellent work in producing this book.

Permission to reprint the following material is gratefully acknowledged:

Selected poems from *The Collected Poems of William Carlos Williams: Volume I, 1909–1939*, edited by A. Walton Litz and Christopher MacGowan. Copyright ©1938 by New Directions Publishing Corporation. Copyright © 1982, 1986 by William Eric Williams and Paul H. Williams. Reprinted by permission of the New Directions Publishing Corporation.

Selected poems from *The Collected Poems of William Carlos Williams: Volume II, 1939–1962*, edited by Christopher MacGowan. Copyright © 1944, 1953; copyright © 1962 by William Carlos Williams. Copyright © 1988 by William Eric Williams and Paul H. Williams. Reprinted by permission of the New Directions Publishing Corporation.

Selected poems from *Collected Early Poems, 1940–1960* by Denise Levertov. Copyright © 1957, 1958, 1959, 1960, 1961, 1979 by Denise Levertov. Reprinted by permission of the New Directions Publishing Corporation.

Selected poems from *Poems, 1960–1967* by Denise Levertov. Copyright © 1958, 1959, 1960, 1961, 1962, 1963, 1964, 1965, 1966 by Denise Levertov. Reprinted by permission of the New Directions Publishing Corporation.

Selected poems from *Collected Poems* by George Oppen. Copyright © 1975 by George Oppen. Reprinted by permission of the New Directions Publishing Corporation.

Selections from "Poem Read at Joan Mitchell's" and "Memorial Day 1950," from *Collected Poems* by Frank O'Hara. Copyright © 1971 by Maureen Granville-Smith. Reprinted by permission of Alfred A. Knopf, Inc.

Selections from "The Day Lady Died," "Personal Poem," and "A Step Away From Them," from *Lunch Poems* by Frank O'Hara. Copyright © 1964 by Frank O'Hara. Reprinted by permission of City Lights Books.

Parts of chapters 2 and 3 were published in different form as "'A Plot of Ground': The Problem of Cultural Identity in the Emergence of Williams' Avant-Garde Stance," *Sagetrieb* 9.3 (winter 1990): 97–119. It is reprinted by permission of the National Poetry Foundation. A condensed version of chapter 5 was published as "The 'Post–Anti-Esthetic' Poetics of Frank O'Hara," *Contemporary Literature* 32.2 (summer 1991): 244–64. It is reprinted by permission of the University of Wisconsin Press.

The American
Avant-Garde
Tradition

1

Introduction: Canon Formation, Avant-Gardism, and William Carlos Williams's Literary Reputation

> In the end Williams may be a token inclusion in a canon that ex-
> cludes what he stands for.
> —Charles Bernstein, "The Academy in Peril:
> William Carlos Williams Meets the MLA"

What *does* Williams stand for? And why has what he stands for mat-
tered so much for post–World War II American poetry? In reiterating
the familiar antipathy between "academic" and "avant-garde" versions
of Williams's literary reputation, Charles Bernstein raises the more
widely contested question of what the field of "modern poetry" stands
for. The extraordinary impact of Williams's poetics on postmodernist
open-form poetry, especially the poetry represented in Donald Allen's
landmark anthology, *The New American Poetry* (1960), is widely acknowledged. Promoted as "our avant-garde, the true continuers of the
modern movement in American poetry,"[1] the New American Poets variously challenged the dominant aesthetic premises of the New Critical
canon, positioning Williams, along with Ezra Pound, as a central figure
in a counterhegemonic American avant-garde "tradition."[2] If Williams's
increased presence in the 1960s academic canon of modern American
poetry was, ironically, impelled by this anti-academic recuperation of
an avant-garde tradition, his academic canonization has accentuated how
this assimilative process tends to decontextualize and therefore defuse
critical avant-garde forms.[3] The formation of Williams's literary reputation has amplified how the politics of cultural memory inform the
construction of literary canons, especially canons of relatively recent
writing, and this heightened awareness of the politics of cultural memory

has characterized Williams's reception by poets and critics alike.[4] However, the significance of the contested terms of his position in American literary history—not only the paradox of an avant-garde "tradition" but also the nationalist designation of this tradition—has not been thoroughly examined.

Because Williams's position in the academic modernist canon has been disputed until only recently, the most influential critical overviews of his career have been those that have argued for his inclusion in this canon on the prevailing formalist terms sanctioned by the New Critical version of modernism, as Peter Schmidt has suggested.[5] Studies of Williams's impact on postwar poetry similarly have tended to rely—at least implicitly—on such canonical standards of value, especially when arguing for the importance of specific poets.[6] In his provocative book-length essay on "recovering" the diversity of modern American poetry, Cary Nelson, like many other critics of the academic canon of American modernism, questions the dominant tendency to reduce literary history to a drama of competition for academic canonization. He argues persuasively that literary history and canon formation should be "separated more distinctly and become contesting cultural forces, with canon formation recognized as necessarily centripetal and elitist and literary history typically centrifugal and democratizing."[7] While Nelson recognizes the canon as an irradicable presence whose centripetal force must nonetheless be resisted, he underestimates how reading is always mediated by canonical standards of value, however conscious a reader may be of such standards.[8] Canon formation can take on a more complex meaning when situated within the problem of literary reputation, rather than as a question of literary value defined primarily by the academy. As John Rodden argues in his impressive study of George Orwell's literary reputation, to speak of "*the* canon" serves the "restrictive view that the traditional high canon of great books is the only canon."[9] Reputation is formed through numerous intersecting "canons," including canons of genres, historical periods, national literatures, literary movements, and aesthetic theories, and thus arises not just from the institutionalization of a writer's texts in school curricula but from the conjunctions and contradictions of intellectual or avant-garde recognition (such as that in literary journals), popular or public recognition (such as that reflected in book sales), and academic recognition. As the public recognition of value, reputation acts as the concealed link between evaluation and interpretation: acts of evaluation serve as the basis for reputations, which in turn are justified by repeated interpretive acts.[10] I would argue that Rodden's thesis applies not only to critical interpretation but to intertextual allusions to writers as well. This is especially true for writers whose reputations are as controversial as Williams's was in the 1950s and 1960s, the period when a renewed debate about the cultural role of the avant-garde—a debate played out in intertextual allusions as well as in critical and polemical writings—marked the paradigm shift from modernism to postmodernism.

As critical theories of postmodernism have variously explained, the decline of the modernist avant-garde coincided with its academic institutionalization as a tradition, especially in the New Critical canon.[11] In one of the most incisive studies of postmodernism, Andreas Huyssen underscores the importance of the reception and institutionalization of modernism—in the academy, as well as in the "burgeoning museum, gallery, concert, record and paperback culture"—for defining the adversarial stance of 1960s postmodernism. Pointing out the irony of the exemplary appeal of the European avant-garde's subversion of high art, he argues that when "for the first time the U.S. had something resembling an 'institution art' in the emphatic European sense, it was modernism itself, the kind of art whose purpose had always been to resist institutionalization."[12] Similarly, Fredric Jameson writes: "One cannot too often symbolically underscore the moment (in most U.S. universities, the late 1950s or 1960s) in which the modern 'classics' entered the school system and the college reading lists. . . . This was a kind of revolution in its own way, with unexpected consequences, forcing the recognition of the modern texts at the same time that it defused them, like former radicals finally appointed to the cabinet."[13] Theoretical overviews of postmodernism such as Huyssen's and Jameson's, which stress how the socioeconomic conditions of consumer capitalism have informed the dissemination of modernist texts, are especially relevant to the reception and transformation of Williams's poetics by postmodernist poets.[14] Such a revised understanding of the dynamics of twentieth-century American literary history also requires a rethinking of the historical and cultural significance of such avant-gardist theories and practices as Williams's in the modernist period as well. To examine how the politics of cultural memory inform the socioaesthetic differences of modernist and postmodernist avant-garde practices of "the Williams tradition," this study concentrates primarily on Williams's positions on and in the "American avant-garde tradition" during two periods in which crucial changes in American cultural identity impelled debates on the national canon: (1) the early modernist period during and after World War I, which marks Williams's emergence as an avant-garde writer at a time of contested literary nationalism, and (2) the period of the paradigm shift from modernism to postmodernism during the late 1950s and 1960s, the cold war and Vietnam War years when Williams's poetics figured so prominently in the poetry "anthology wars" fought over the meaning of modernism.

The initial chapters of this study demonstrate how two dominant rhetorical motives structure Williams's responsiveness to cultural change: what I call his "poetics of descent" and his "poetics of dissent." As the son of immigrants himself, and as a physician who served subsequent immigrants, Williams's writing is especially sensitive to the widespread experience of dislocation. His experimental forms contest not only the hegemony of the English literary tradition in American culture but, like the work of many of his contemporaries, contest the central position of the New England past for American national identity. To resist the ide-alizing impulse of "puritanism," to counteract especially its denigration of the body, Williams foregrounds the material act of articulation. *In the American Grain*, for example, repeatedly reflects on the discursive act of rewriting the past. His early lyric poetry enacts this process even more autobiographically, as he mediates his immigrant filiations and avant-garde affiliations through intertextual constructions of a multi-cultural New World literary "descent." His poetics furthermore "dissent" from any grounds for defining an American poetic language in terms that outlaw the heteroglossia of speech types (marking differences of class, ethnicity, race, gender, profession, region, etc.) from literary dis-course. His poetic forms exemplify what M. M. Bakhtin defines as the "novelistic hybrid": "an artistically organized system for bringing dif-ferent languages in contact with one another, a system having as its goal the illumination of one language by means of another."[15] By recontextual-izing genres such as the dramatic monologue, the pastoral, and the imagist lyric, Williams's "novelistic" appropriation of poetic forms ques-tions conventional expectations that poetic discourse transcends every-day life. Such experimental forms act as what Richard Terdiman would call "counter-discourses"[16]—they relativize the authority and stability of poetic genres as they self-reflexively foreground the situated act of articulation that makes up the lyric utterance.

Williams's writing answers both the shared "international" experience

of modernity (the unprecedented experience of the ephemerality, fragmentation, and contingency of everyday life) and the specifically "national" experience of extraordinary demographic change resulting from
the growth of industrialism and urbanization. His commitment to experimentation and the destruction of traditional forms allied his poetics with the critical stance of the European avant-garde. As Peter Bürger
has argued in his influential formulation of the historical avant-garde,
such movements as dada, surrealism, and futurism shared a goal of reinte-
grating art with social praxis in challenging the function of art's autonomy. In proclaiming themselves as artificial constructs, self-critical texts
such as Marcel Duchamp's ready-mades implicitly critiqued the systems of production, distribution, and reception of artwork, thus making "art as an institution" recognizable.[17]

Williams's notion of literary production concurs in many ways with
the more overtly political formulations of Walter Benjamin. Citing
Brecht's epic theater as his primary example, Benjamin writes in 1934:
"*An author who teaches writers nothing, teaches no one.* What matters,
therefore, is the exemplary character of production, which is able first
to induce other producers to produce, and second to put an approved
apparatus at their disposal. And this apparatus is better the more consumers it is able to turn into producers—that is, readers or spectators
into collaborators."[18] Although skeptical of Marxist dialectics, Williams,
like Benjamin and Brecht, foregrounds technique as the means for turn-
ing consumers into producers, readers into collaborators. In his critical
writings on those modern writers whose technique he most admired,
Williams continually reiterates how experimentation with literary form
and language can initiate a "break through all preconception of poetic
form and mood and pace, a crack in the bowl," demonstrating how "destruction and creation are simultaneous."[19] When the word, the phrase,
the sentence, or even the generic form is situated in a radically new,
even obscure, context, its connection to the modern world is not oblit-
erated, but accentuated: "Good modern work, far from being the fragmentary, neurotic thing its disunderstanders think it, is nothing more
than work compelled by those conditions. It is a multiplicity of impulses that by their several flights, crossing at all eccentric angles, *might*
enlighten."[20] Such writing reintegrates art with social praxis by leaving
sequences of fragments open to supplementary responses, thus producing
a clearer understanding of modern fragmentation. Marianne Moore's
poems, for example, are neither mimetic reflections of the "fragmentary

neurotic" world nor autonomous aesthetic forms that transcend everyday life. Her poems occupy a " 'special' place," but this place is the same
"as that where bricks or colored thread are handled."[21] Similarly, a text
like *Ulysses*, because of its "broken words" and fractured syntax, "forces"
one "to separate the words from the printed page, to take them up into
a world where the imagination is at play and where the words are no
more than titles under the illustrations." But this "world" of imaginative play illuminates the social conditions from which it arises: "It is the
modern world emerging among the living ancients by paying attention
to the immediacy of its own contact."[22] This cognitive process—from
the printed page, to the imagination "at play," to the re-cognition that
such play elucidates the writer's "contact" with his locality—inverts the
critical premises of aestheticism. Rather than the ascent from the local
to the transcendent category of the aesthetic, Williams stresses the descent from the realm of the aesthetic to the reformulation of the local
conditions that give rise to such imaginative work.

Although he shared the European avant-gardist goal of integrating
art into the praxis of life, Williams articulated his commitment to the
local and the quotidian, especially in his use of working-class speech
types and other discourses traditionally excluded from lyric poetry, as a
distinctively American anti-elitist response to modernization. Williams's
conceptualization of an Americanist avant-garde was paradoxical, as *In
the American Grain*, "The American Background," and the essays for
Contact, for example, demonstrate. What distinguishes his project from
both Duchamp's dadaist anti-aesthetics and Eliot's high modernist aesthetics is his insistence on a "localist" avant-gardism, which correlates
indigenous diction and forms with the rejection of European aesthetic
models. As one of Williams's finest readers, the British poet Charles
Tomlinson, has summarized, locality is not just the geographic source
of Williams's poetics but the source of his lineation as well, "the jerks
and outbursts of speech rendered on the here and now of the page." If
Williams's sense of locality begins with "a somatic awareness, a physiological presence in time and space,"[23] then his project for returning art
to everyday life impels his examination of the social conditions transforming the modern subject's relation to time and space. This project
informs the linguistic, formal, and rhetorical experimentation of his critical avant-garde stance that is simultaneously aware of the social texts
that constitute his locality.

Williams's appeal to experimental poets as diverse as Louis Zukofsky,

George Oppen, Charles Olson, and Robert Creeley, Allen Ginsberg, Frank O'Hara, Diane Wakoski, and Denise Levertov can be attributed to his Americanist avant-garde rhetorical stance. His sustained opposition to the elitist assumptions of high modernism, especially to its insistence on preserving the autonomy of art in a canonical tradition, became increasingly relevant as the academic hegemony of the New Criticism appeared to foreclose any links between poetry and politics. The Black Mountain poets, the New York poets, the San Francisco poets, and the earlier generation of objectivist poets, among others, cited Williams's poetic theory and practice in their polemical writings to challenge New Critical doctrine, which, with its aestheticist separation of poetry from history, was seen to be complicit with the dominant cold-war ideology.[24] While the prominence of his poetics grew for experimental poets and editors of little magazines in the 1950s, his copious postwar output compelled a reevaluation by even those critics who had previously neglected his achievement. With the ongoing publication of *Paterson* (1946–51), with the publication of his *Collected Later Poems* (1950), *Collected Earlier Poems* (1951), *Make Light of It: Collected Stories* (1950), *Autobiography* (1951), *Selected Essays* (1954), and several new volumes of lyric poems, the prewar stereotype of the antipoetic, tough sentimentalist could no longer account for the diversity of his writing. As Paul Mariani has written, some reviewers thought that Williams was "like the person who sticks around after his own bon voyage party, reemerging periodically and causing no end of embarrassment."[25] As he continued to experiment with poetic forms and genres, Williams's place in American literary history became a site for struggle, a struggle in which he himself vigorously participated, as exemplified by numerous reviews and introductions of younger poets, as well as by such symbolic acts of public recognition as the adoption of Ginsberg as a poetic "son" in *Paterson* and the quotations of Olson's "Projective Verse" in his *Autobiography*, Gilbert Sorrentino's prose in *Paterson*, and, more problematically, Marcia Nardi's letters in *Paterson*.[26] Such an active role in defining his legacy itself divided Williams's readers: as James Breslin has written, Williams came to be recognized by the more familiar caricatures of either "the affectionate, tolerant, and homespun patron saint of contemporary poetry" or the "mindlessly indiscriminate zealot ready and willing to write a puff at the drop of a chapbook."[27] Even for those poets who found Williams's overlapping tropes of "descent" and "dissent" especially appropriate for responding to the historical conditions of postmodernity, the homologies that he assumed—a democratic social philosophy with a poetics of free verse and open forms, and a commitment to the local with an antagonistic stance toward poetic tradition—nevertheless became more problematic in the light of postwar American nationalism.

In his introduction to the Language poetry anthology whose title echoes Williams's quest for a "usable past," *In the American Tree*, Ron Silliman writes that the only points of agreement that unite the heterogeneous poetics of the New American Poetry are "an insistence on the centrality of the influence of William Carlos Williams and a preference for poetry that, read aloud, sounded spoken."[28] Williams was most often cited by poets in the 1950s and '60s precisely *because* of his attention to the rhythms and syntax of spoken language. He represented an accessible alternative to the conservative position on poetic language articulated by T. S. Eliot: "We cannot, in literature, any more than in the rest of life, live in a perpetual state of revolution. If every generation of poets made it their task to bring poetic diction up to date with the spoken language, poetry would fail in one of its most important obligations. For poetry should help, not only to refine the language of the time, but to prevent it from changing too rapidly: a development of language at too great a speed would be a development in the sense of a progressive deteriorization, and that is our danger today."[29] Denise Levertov spoke for many of her contemporaries in her commemoration of Williams in the *Nation*, claiming that Williams's most important legacy was his opening "the whole range of the language," the "recognition of wide resources."[30] For example, when asked in a 1960 interview about Williams's poetics, LeRoi Jones (now Amiri Baraka) noted that Williams had taught him "how to write in my own language—how to write the way I *speak* rather than the way I *think* a poem ought to be written."[31] The most frequent tributes to Williams's liberating effects on younger writers explain how his use of everyday spoken language fosters formal experimentation. Allen Ginsberg recalls that after hearing Williams read, he experienced a "revelation of absolute common sense." He found Williams's poetry to have "a meaning which is identical with its form, with a rhythm identical with the arrangement of the words on the page, and the words on the page arranged identically with what you want to say and how you want to say it."[32] Robert Creeley, although less hyperbolic than Ginsberg, follows Williams in explaining the integration of his form and content as the embodiment of the historical conditions distinguishing American speech from "English." The act of discovering form in process is analogous to American speech because Americans "have had both to imagine and thereby to make that reality which they are given to live in. It is as though they had to *realize* the world.[33]

Such convergent accounts of Williams's poetics by poets of such divergent idioms testifies to the significance of his insistence on poetry's responsiveness to linguistic change. This insistence has enabled rather than inhibited those poets who have modeled themselves after Williams, as Gilbert Sorrentino's recollection exemplifies: "My slow understanding of Williams' work exhilarated and depressed me—the former since I saw in his writing a method of anchoring his work sans stuffiness and dullness, the latter because I realized that Williams was not a peer; there was something that I 'heard' that Williams did not."[34] Sorrentino's remark indicates a generational difference that distances Williams's "American idiom" from the idiom of younger poets. Such a difference is inevitable for those who follow Williams's example of renewing the language through poetry, but it also indicates a skepticism toward programmatic definitions of poetic language. Creeley's reiteration of Williams's Americanist explanation of linguistic difference is somewhat misleading, for the "American idiom" has generally been more meaningful for writers whose sociolinguistic affiliations have made them more sensitive to social variations in American English. Robert Duncan indirectly alludes to this in explaining why he was *not* interested in Williams's theories of American speech: "Williams, you see, kept feeling that he really wasn't American. We find out that his grandmother spoke Spanish, so he had to stake a claim on the American language. Well, I couldn't possibly talk any language that wasn't American, because I happen to be, I think, twelfth-generation American."[35] As Duncan suggests, the multilingual immigrant background of Williams's family, as well as his work with immigrant and working-class patients, made him acutely aware of the social registers of American English. Yet whereas Levertov, Jones, Ginsberg, Creeley, and Sorrentino variously cite the importance of Williams's formal attention to the act of enunciation, his programmatic appeal to the "American idiom" reifies the dynamic qualities that distinguish his poetic use of spoken language.

If Williams's linguistic experimentation had produced innovative forms responsive to historical change, his postwar arguments for such concepts as the "American idiom" and the "variable foot" were as consistently insistent as they were idiomatic and variable. Randall Jarrell, who wrote the laudatory introduction to Williams's *Selected Poems* (1949), several years later sardonically criticized the cultural nationalist stance of his polemics:

> America is his own family, so that he says awful things about it but cannot bear for anyone else to; and he is always saying, too, that it is better than everything. But he is ill at ease in Zion, both in our republic and in the republic of letters; he looks at the poets along his street in time more distrustfully, though, than he looks at the people along his street in Paterson. He is as American as even he himself could wish, and cannot resist constantly bringing up (in the poems themselves, often) the "problem" of how American poets should write poetry, and answering that they must *be* modern and *be* American. He might as well wish for the nineteenth century to be over.[36]

Although Jarrell's dismissal of Williams's concern with the "American idiom" is sarcastic, it exemplifies the rancor that Williams's combative polemics aroused even among those who were sympathetic to his poetry.[37] The question of cultural identity preoccupied Williams throughout his career, but cultural nationalism certainly had different political implications in the post–World War II years of *Paterson* than it had during the post–World War I years of *In the American Grain*. Post–World War II cultural nationalism was predicated on the kind of assertions of the uniqueness of American culture that informed *In the American Grain*; however, the consumer culture of the fifties more forcefully imposed conformity and standardization as the ideal "American way of life," repressing social difference. This ideal of a homogeneous culture coincided with the more internationalist, expansionist definition of cultural identity, a paradigm shift that David Noble has called "the end of American history," i.e., the end of an exceptionalist history. With the concurrent impact of cold-war politics and economic expansion, the progressivist belief that the growth of capitalism threatened participatory democracy was no longer widely affirmed. The shift among liberal historians from the progressive model to the consensus model of American history, for example, assumed a dissociation of economic progress from political progress. The impact of this dissociation on American national consciousness would not be fully felt until the Vietnam War years. However, the cultural contradictions coinciding with the declining exceptionalist myth altered the political significance of Williams's appeal for an Americanist avant-garde poetics.

Williams's repeated defense of the "American idiom" was of course also a campaign to ensure a legacy for his poetics. But his constant appeal to the literary canon, frequently personified as Eliot, reinserts value as the dominant issue for literary production, overshadowing the more complex political question that his poetics foreground, the question of access to linguistic means of expression, spoken or written. John Guillory has recently argued that the question of literacy underlies the current debate on canon formation. Principles of exclusion are meaningless without considering how institutional structures regulate access to literacy. Guillory's claim that "there is no theoretical understanding of the relation between a historical silence—exclusion from the means of literary production—and the sphere of reception, where texts confront readers as simply given, as already speaking the language of literate culture" is especially germane to "the Williams tradition."[38] Williams's intertextual strategies for revising the canon of American literature were compelled by his sensitivity to such "historical silence." However, he articulates the cultural politics of such exclusion in the limiting terms of national traditions. Guillory notes that although "the vernacular canon as a pseudo-scripture takes its place in the ideology of national traditions," the more profound "social effects of standardizing vernacular speech" are often ignored. He argues that "an elite literary language may be the basis for this standard, but not its determinant."[39] Williams's Americanist argument against British English as an elite literary language exemplifies the position that Guillory questions. Although certainly sensitive to the socioeconomic bases of linguistic differentiation, Williams's nationalistic conception of literary language and tradition becomes the main source of contention for articulating the political effects of his poetics.

In what is probably the most frequently cited summary of Williams's poetics—his introduction to his 1944 volume *The Wedge*—he asserts that "there is no poetry of distinction without formal invention, for it is in the intimate form that works of art achieve their exact meaning, in which they most resemble the machine, to give language its highest dignity, its illumination in the environment to which it is native."[40] To write innovative poetry, then, the poet must meet the linguistic demands of his or her immediate time and place. Or, to transpose what he says about Whitman in "America, Whitman and the Art of Poetry," the only way to write like Williams is to write *unlike* Williams. This paradox informs the reception and transformation of Williams's poetics by postwar open-form poets. The three poets whom I have chosen to analyze in the second part of this study—Denise Levertov, Frank O'Hara, and George Oppen—are each especially, although quite differently, attuned not only to the paradox of an avant-garde tradition but also to sociolinguistic variations of American English. Each influentially extends Williams's principles of poetic language and form to respond to the historical conditions of postmodernity by inverting Williams's modernist dictum: the only way to write unlike Williams is to write *like* Williams but to foreground the intertextual act of doing so. I have also selected these poets from the many possible choices because their affiliations with Williams's poetics have not been studied as thoroughly as have, for example, those of Robert Creeley, Charles Olson, or Allen Ginsberg. Problematic figures in "the canon" of postwar poetry themselves, these poets raise significant questions about the cultural politics of situating Williams in the center of the American "avant-garde tradition." Unlike many of their contemporaries, each furthermore challenges the Americanist and masculinist assumptions of Williams's poetic stance, while investigating the rhetoric of centrality and marginality that informs academic and avant-garde canon formation.

2

"A Plot of Ground": Williams's Poetics of Descent

Williams . . . certainly has made a splendid struggle to plasticize all his various selves and he is perhaps more people at once than anyone I've ever known—not vague persons but he's a small town of serious citizens in himself. I never saw so many defined human beings in one being. That's because he's latin and anglo-saxon in several divisions and he being an artist has to give them all a chance.
—Marsden Hartley, letter to Alfred Stieglitz, 9 October 1923

If he goes to France, it is not to learn a *do re mi fa sol.* He goes to see a strange New World.

If not definitely a culture new in every part, at least a satisfaction. He wants to have the feet of his understanding on the ground, his ground, *the* ground, the only ground that he knows, that which *is* under his feet. I speak of aesthetic satisfaction. This want, in America, can only be filled by knowledge, a poetic knowledge, of that ground.
—William Carlos Williams, *In the American Grain*

William Carlos Williams's "splendid struggle to plasticize all his various selves" has produced repeated attempts to locate *the* Williams amid the multiplicity of his literary projects. Whether charting these "various selves," arguing for the predominance of one such self, or positing the principles that "plasticize" these selves, Williams's readers have had to account for the multifarious contradictions that disrupt any unified construction of his poetic stance. Marsden Hartley's letter to Alfred Stieglitz typifies the predominant modernist rhetorical strategy for "grounding" Williams's early personae in an integrated portrait of the artist. In foregrounding Williams's "latin and anglo-saxon" descent as the reason for his plasticity, Hartley introduces the discourse of nationality

25

that divides the "ethnic" and the "American." And in settling on the artist as the category that transcends Williams's "divisions," Hartley translates Williams's multiethnic descent into an asset for "international" modernist artistic production. The mixture of "latin" and "anglo-saxon" genealogies becomes a ready-made recipe for producing syncretic literary forms. The rhetoric of Hartley's portrait anticipates formalist "plots" for locating Williams in the Anglo-American modernist literary canon, but it also parallels the historicist "plots" for locating Williams's "feet" on the American "ground." Like the aesthetic category of the artist, the national category of the American transcends the "divisions" of Williams's "descent," both literary and genealogical, that animate his hybrid forms during and after World War I.

This chapter analyzes how Williams reconciled his immigrant filiations and modernist affiliations through intertextual constructions of an American literary "descent." The figure of "descent" that Williams invoked in his Samuel Houston chapter in *In the American Grain* to "ground" the "New World" poet recurs throughout his writing as a trope of renewal, a quest for origins or "ground" that presupposes an initial dislocation or displacement. This trope is most evident in Williams's variations of the Kora legend (e.g., in *Kora in Hell*), but it also informs later figures found in *Paterson* such as the "radiant gist" and the "Beautiful Thing," so frequently cited to define the "ground" of his poetics. As Joseph Riddell argues in *The Inverted Bell*, however, these figures do not signify a transcendent center but the central problematic of Williams's poetry: the "ground" itself is a problem of interpretation. Whereas Riddell broadly situates Williams's poetics within the Homeric tradition, my point of departure for examining the relation of poetic form and "ground" in Williams's early poetics is the specific question of American cultural identity that his immigrant family background accentuates. I will examine in detail three texts that self-consciously dramatize Williams's emergence as an American writer: two poems from his 1917 collection *Al Que Quire!* ("January Morning" and "Dedication to a Plot of Ground") and one prose narrative from *In the American Grain* (1925) ("Père Sebastien Rasles"). In these autobiographical texts, Williams does not break with family, ethnic background, class, and community. Instead, he follows a pattern familiar to ethnic American writing: writing from a marginal position between the dominant and minority cultures, his rhetorical strategies bridge the differences between his filiative and affiliative relationships.

Hartley's strategy for translating Williams's multiethnic "descent" into aesthetic terms typifies interpretations of Williams that argue for his international perspective, but it also typifies those that argue for his American perspective. For example, Ezra Pound, one of Williams's earliest supporters, summarized his national "position" in a 1928 review of his prose for the *Dial:*

> Carlos Williams has been determined to stand or sit as an American. Freud would probably say "because his father was English" (in fact half English, half Danish). His mother, as ethnologists have before noted, was a mixture of French and Spanish. Of late years (the last four or five) Dr. Williams has laid claim to a somewhat remote Hebrew connexion, possibly a rabbi in Saragossa, at the time of the siege. He claims American birth, but I strongly suspect that he emerged on shipboard just off Bedloe's Island and that his dark and serious eyes gazed up in their first sober contemplation at the statue and its brazen and monstrous nightshirt.[1]

Like Hartley, Pound implies that although genealogy to some extent does determine one's "perspective," nationality and even genealogy can be construed as fictions that one can manipulate. Not only does Pound emphasize the element of choice in Williams's nationality, but he suggests that "his remote Hebrew connexion" is also an artist's construct, one that reinforces Williams's position as "an observant foreigner." Certainly Freud would have something to say about Pound's genealogical portrait of Williams, but in stressing Williams's immigrant background, Pound makes an insistent case for the aesthetic value of seeing America as "something interesting *but exterior.*"[2] In arguing that Williams's position on the margins of American culture informs the authenticity of his aesthetic vision, Pound conflates the genealogical, historical marginality of the "ethnic" immigrant with the geographical marginality of the European explorer scanning the shore of the New World.

Pound's portrait of the immigrant artist as international modernist oddly parallels the rhetoric of arguments that stress the "American" qualities of Williams's poetry. For example, Paul Rosenfeld's assessment of Williams in *Port of New York*, the first book to read Williams's poetry alongside comparable New York avant-garde innovations in music and the visual arts, appears to be antithetical to Pound's interpretation of Williams's internationalist perspective. Comparing Williams to Eliot, Rosenfeld claims that Williams's poems "give the relationship of things more justly than do the emigre's. . . . He can give himself, William Carlos Williams, much as he is, without either simple or inverted pride; give himself in his crassness, in his dissonant mixed blood, in absurd melancholy, wild swiftness of temper, man-shyness; Americano, Jerseyite, Rutherfordian; give himself with a frankness, a fearlessness, a scientific impersonality, that is bracing as a shock of needle-spray."[3] The rhetoric of Rosenfeld's portrait, one long sentence whose verb and object are interrupted by the battery of short descriptive phrases, careens toward a conclusion not substantially different than Pound's portrait of the "observant foreigner." While the descriptive phrases accumulate the distinct characteristics of Williams's aesthetic vision, attributing his dynamic, temperamental personality to both his genealogy ("his dissonant mixed blood," "Americano") and his suburban residence ("Jerseyite, Rutherfordian"), this character sketch concludes with the emphasis on Williams's "scientific impersonality." Like Pound, like Hartley, Rosenfeld implies that the genealogical and geographical differences that inform Williams's aesthetic vision are subsumed in the aesthetic moment.

Williams's readers have tended to follow his lead in submerging his genealogical "divisions" into an American division within modernist poetics. However, such attention to his "latin and anglo-saxon" selves as Hartley's, Pound's, and Rosenfeld's represents a typical modernist preoccupation with ethnic and cultural difference. The question of American cultural identity, accompanying an increased international role after World War I, manifested itself in the intensely debated issue of literary nationalism and very much informed Williams's emergence as a writer. The problem of immigration was central to this debate about literary nationalism, and as Marcus Klein describes, it has structured lasting divisions within literary modernism:

> What had been a facsimile of culture was chaos within which everybody was a foreigner, including the native-born and the millions of authentic foreigners. And there were consequences for the making of literature. Having no culture in which to be at home, writers made one—or, rather, they fabricated many versions of a culture depending on their various kinds of knowledge of what they had been dispossessed from and reasonably they could come into possession of. . . . Not unreasonably . . . children of the Mayflower tended to invent Western culture, and children of the immigrants tended to invent America.[4]

The increasingly multiethnic composition of the United States population was in fact the pivotal issue for defining American cultural identity. As the influx of southern and eastern European immigrants during the 1900s and 1910s was challenging the nineteenth-century ideal of a mixed, assimilating nationality, the concept of unrestricted immigration was no longer so widely accepted. The entrance of the United States into World War I increased the pressure for national unity and homogeneity, fueling the climate of xenophobia, intolerance, and repression that culminated in the 1919 "Red Scare." From the Espionage Act of 1917 through the immigrant restriction acts of the early twenties, federal and state governments instituted policies of Americanization and deportation that reflected the increasingly nativist character of nationalism. World War I nationalism did provoke the counterformation of a cosmopolitan ideal of intellect—the urban, ethnically diverse, anti-provincial ideal familiarly known as the "New York intellectual" tradition. However, the rise of nationalism also resulted in a more homogenized notion of the American literary past in academia, as American literature was for the first time becoming institutionalized in the university as an independent subject of study. As literary scholarship became professionalized, constructions of American literary history began to incorporate the nationalist and formalist direction of literary studies. While the search for a "usable past" resulted in an emphasis on texts that revealed American culture, the aestheticist criteria for evaluating these texts narrowed the canon of American writers. The definition of "American literature" was becoming increasingly restricted to those texts that were judged as transcending historical interest.[5]

Edward Said's analysis of the tensions between "filiation" and "affiliation" among modernist writers is especially helpful for differentiating Williams's emergence as a writer from that of many of his contemporaries. Said has argued that the careers of many modernist writers, such as Joyce, Lawrence, and Pound, have followed a three-part pattern of movement from biological filiation toward cultural affiliation.[6] The pattern begins with the rejection of ties with family, class, country, and traditional beliefs in order to achieve spiritual and economic freedom. This break from a failed idea or possibility of filiation leads to the embracement of a compensatory order, such as a political party, an institution, a culture, or a set of beliefs. This "affiliative mode of relationship" consequently reinstates the authority associated with the former filiative order. Said's formulation perhaps best describes the career of Williams's adversary, T. S. Eliot, but it also illuminates his countermovement toward an Americanist poetics. In demonstrating how this three-part pattern structures literary knowledge in the academy, i.e., in the maintenance of a canon and in the process of professionalization, Said identifies the issues that motivated Williams's virulent opposition not only to Eliot himself but to the general academic reception of modern poetry. Said's argument also helps explain such interpretive schemes as Hartley's that foreshadow the academic assimilation of Williams's poetry into the American modernist canon. However, his distinction between filiation and affiliation is especially problematic for the emergent modernist writer's process of reconciling his multiethnic immigrant family background with the changing conceptions of American cultural identity during the early decades of the century. As Dickran Tashjian has pointed out, modernism in the United States after the Armory Show was linked with the conception of immigrants as foreigners who needed to be domesticated.[7] The acceptance of modernism involved an assimilation of new aesthetic forms to the experiences of American society. This process of assimilation applied not only to American culture in general but to the American artist, whose aesthetic "rite of passage" from the old to the new was analogous to the "symbolic transformation" of immigrants.[8] Like the immigrant's, the artist's transformation was inevitably disruptive, requiring a reintegration of the self changed in passage.

The tension between Williams's ethnic filiations and his avant-garde affiliations dominated his early construction of a literary identity, as the indecision over his choice of authorial signature for his first two books indicates. He omitted "Carlos" in his first book, *Poems* (1909), settling on "William C. Williams." He then included "Carlos" for the signature of his second book, *The Tempers* (1913). This book was furthermore dedicated to the man after whom "Carlos" was named, his mother's brother, Carlos Hoheb, who had practiced medicine in Puerto Rico and Haiti.[9] Williams's next book, *Al Que Quire!*, is often cited as the collection in which he discovered his characteristic poetic "voice," and the background of its title alone testifies to the heteroglossia of this voice. Williams explained in a letter to Marianne Moore that he wanted to call his book *A Book of Poems: Al Que Quiere!*:

—which means: To him who wants it—but I like the Spanish just as I like a Chinese image cut out of stone: it is decorative and has a certain integral charm. But such a title is not democratic—does not truly represent the contents of the book, so I have added:

A Book of Poems
AL QUE QUIRE!
or
THE PLEASURES OF DEMOCRACY[10]

Williams's explanation for his choice of title reveals the mixture of motives that characterize this collection. The Spanish title—which actually does not contain the object Williams translates as "it"—puns on *want*, as the book offers poems to those readers who desire (and choose) to read them, while simultaneously mocking those who lack (and/or reject) what these poems have to offer. This double sense of want, which assumes the probability of his audience's resistance, whether in the form of outright rejection or of just not getting "it," arises mainly from the book's sexual themes. However, Williams's letter also indicates that this presumed resistance is related to the book's aesthetic forms, beginning with its title. Without an identifiable rhetorical situation, this declarative statement in Spanish becomes an imagist construct. But the terms describing this construct suggest Williams's conflicting interpretations of the value of a purely aesthetic object. It is "decorative," having no instrumental value, but by its "certain integral charm" its aesthetic value as a self-contained object can be affirmed. Each of these conflicting interpretations of the title as aesthetic object assumes that the use of a Spanish title for an American book of poems is aristocratic, "not democratic." Thus the opposition of aestheticism and democracy revolves around the third term, the Spanish quotation signifying the ethnic other. The Spanish language familiar to Williams from his childhood is also the language of the book's epigraph, a passage from a story by the Guatemalan writer Rafael Arévale Martínez. Prominently displayed in the book's title, however, the Spanish language becomes objectified "like a Chinese image cut out of stone."

The publisher of *Al Que Quiere!*, Edmund Brown, disapproved of Williams's subtitle, so it was removed. However, the publisher's dustjacket blurb transforms the doubts linking title to subtitle into quite another version of the "democratic" book of poems:

> To Whom It May Concern! This book is a collection of poems by William Carlos Williams. You, gentle reader, will probably not like it, because it is brutally powerful and scornfully crude. Fortunately, neither the author nor the publisher care [*sic*] much whether you like it or not. The author has done his work, and if you *do* read the book you will agree that he doesn't give a damn for your opinion. . . . We have the profound

satisfaction of publishing a book in which, we venture to predict, the
poets of the future will dig for material as the poets of today dig in
Whitman's *Leaves of Grass*. (CP 1, 480)

Rather than as a "Chinese image cut out of stone," *Al Que Quire!* now
functions quite differently: it marks the iconoclastic, macho primitive
as Hispanic-American poet of democracy. Promoted as a sensationalis-
tic and threatening collection, this book of "brutally powerful and scornfully crude" poems is avant-garde in its confrontational, destructive
stance. Yet it is simultaneously traditional in its "democratic" values,
the natural successor to Whitman's epic poem of American nationality.
The dialectic of the aesthetic and the democratic, the imagist and the
Whitmanesque, generates the multiple contradictions constituting
Williams's early poetic stance. Combining the "decorative" with the
"brutally powerful and scornfully crude," *Al Que Quiere!* exemplifies
the range of Williams's early experimentation; its public and private
modes of address coexist even within individual poems. Although antagonistic toward its readers and aggressively defensive of its aesthetic
pretensions, this volume persistently affirms the perspective of marginality shared by such "democratic" subjects as women, children, the elderly, ethnic minorities, and the working class. It is no idle coincidence
that Williams's publisher invokes *Leaves of Grass* as a point of comparison, for *Al Que Quire!* affirms the openness of Whitman's poetic stance
while revising his open poetic form.

Williams takes up the question of Whitman's importance for modern American poetry in "America, Whitman and the Art of Poetry"
(1917). In this essay he claims that Whitman is "our rock, our first primitive. We cannot advance until we have grasped Whitman and then built
upon him."[11] If Whitman represents the "pinnacle" of American poetry, he also stands as an "edifice" whose imposing presence must not
only be "grasped" but resisted. Williams indicates his own strategy for
dealing with Whitman's colossal presence:

The only way to be like Whitman is to write *unlike* Whitman. Do I ex-
pect to be a companion to Whitman by mimicking his manners? I might
even so please some old dotard, some "good grey poet" by kow-towing
to him; but not to Whitman—or if I did please Whitman I would not
please myself. Let me at least realize that to be a poet one must be himself!
    What have I done now! "Be himself?" What the devil difference does
it make to anyone whether a man is himself or not as long as he write

good poetry. "Be a Whitman, if you will, only please, if you love your kind, *don't write like Whitman*."[12]

The dialogical process of self-correction—the abrupt transition from "one must be himself" to "What have I done now!"—suggests one method for writing unlike Whitman. The Whitmanesque "I," which enacts the nationalist vision of assimilation, becomes the "I" that sustains its "divisions" or that "fidgets with point of view." In positing a split between "being" and writing, Williams opens the possibility for incorporating the style and idealism of Whitman, while still experimenting with new poetic forms and more realistic modes of presenting modern subjects. Williams resists Whitman's idealizing nationalism, but he appropriates his insistence on the "American language" to focus on "local" linguistic structures and "local" experience.[13] We can trace this process of being a Whitman, but writing unlike him, most explicitly in "January Morning."

"January Morning" recalls "Crossing Brooklyn Ferry" in its language and in its subject, as it records the poet's journey across the Hudson between Manhattan and New Jersey. However, the structure of this poem, a "suite" of fifteen short sections in various rhetorical modes, looks forward to the cubist polyphonic collage of such poetic sequences as *Spring and All*, *The Descent of Winter*, and *Della Primavera Trasportata al Morale* more than it looks back to Whitman. "January Morning" begins with the poet's localization of the "beauties of travel," as he argues that the familiar can be aesthetically appreciated when perceived in unfamiliar conditions:

> I have discovered that most of
> the beauties of travel are due to
> the strange hours we keep to see them:
>
> the domes of the Church of
> the Paulist Fathers in Weehawken
> against a smoky dawn—the heart stirred—
> are beautiful as Saint Peters
> approached after years of anticipation.
>
> (*CP 1*, 100)

Using a familiar Wordsworthian trope to describe a defamiliarized scene, this vision of Weehawken nevertheless affirms the aesthetic value of New World spontaneity, contrasted to the more rational Old World "anticipation." The poem then proceeds to describe what the poet sees in the early morning urban streets with a sequence of descriptive predicate clauses, each beginning with "and," following the initial "I saw." The paratactic syntax and oratorical free verse rhythm resembles Whitman, but there is a significant difference: each of the seven predicate clauses is a separately numbered stanza. This series of self-contained vignettes transforms Whitman's catalog into a series of imagist lyrics. The first half of "January Morning" sustains a coherent, realistic narrative, but the numbered sequence of vignettes produces the effect of a series of snapshots. This sequence can be viewed more mimetically as interrupted glimpses recorded from the poet's train-window vantage point.[14] This method of juxtaposing images becomes more complex when the narrative itself becomes fragmented, as the poem begins to juxtapose varying speech acts:

> —and the rickety ferry-boat "Arden"!
> What an object to be called "Arden"
> among the great piers,—on the
> ever new river!
>
> > "Put me a Touchstone
> > at the wheel, white gulls, and we'll
> > follow the ghost of the Half Moon
> > to the North West Passage—and through!
> > (at Albany!) for all that!"
>
> (CP 1, 102)

This stanza deviates from the realistic description of the previous stanzas, as its reference to Shakespeare's *As You Like It* imparts an aura of romance to the ferry journey. This reference to Williams's frequently cited exemplar for timeless literary excellence is supplemented by references to voyages that are historically and geographically closer to Williams. The "ever new river" may be read as an echo of Heraclitus or as a metaphor for the experience of modernity, but Williams's affirmation of his own local knowledge, his ability to read this "ever new river," also evokes Twain's Mississippi River pilots. The reference to the *Half Moon* reaffirms such realistic use of detail as Twain's, as romantic or even fantastic as it sounds, for it recalls a voyage by Henry Hudson himself, the explorer whose name imparts a historical continuity to the "ever new river." However, Williams takes up where Hudson left off ("to the North West Passage—and through!"), for the *Half Moon* was

Hudson's ship for a voyage of exploration that he abandoned at Albany.[15] This reference to Hudson's voyage toward the North West Passage furthermore evokes Whitman's affirmation of American exploration and expansion, especially the optimistic nationalism of "Passage to India." Finally, this passage marks a transition from the first-person narrative to a mixed mode of address. Among these modes is the mode of address that appears in quotation marks in the extract; it is a problematic mode for modern poetry, the mode of apostrophe. The use of apostrophe here and later in "January Morning" makes this poem's invocation of Whitman more parodic than imitative.

The poet quotes himself when he tells the "white gulls" to "Put me a Touchstone / at the wheel," thus distancing himself from the apostrophic act. However, the poem goes on to address the "Exquisite brown waves" in language reminiscent of "Crossing Brooklyn Ferry." This apostrophic mode plays a crucial role in Williams's transformation of the Whitmanesque lyric "I" in "January Morning." Jonathan Culler has argued that the use of apostrophe epitomizes the lyric's difference from other genres. Apostrophe functions in post-Enlightenment poetry as a strategy for overcoming the alienation of subject from object. Invoking the orphic power of poetry to make objects responsive forces, apostrophe enacts a process of subject-object reconciliation by making the object function as a subject. Unlike narrative, lyric apostrophe locates events in the present, removing the opposition of absence and presence from empirical time and locating it in discursive time. Apostrophe thus produces a fictive, discursive event, rather than the representation of an event. However, Culler also notes that apostrophe, as the "sign of a fiction which knows its fictive nature," can also be read as an act of radical interiorization or solipsism.[16] The rarity of usage of apostrophe in modern poetry can be attributed to anxiety about such solipsism.

By interrupting the narrative description of "January Morning" with an apostrophic address, Williams dramatizes the performative aspect of poetry. But the apostrophic passages of this poem so resemble Whitman that they function almost as quotations, as texts inserted into a cubist collage, rather than as the lyric speaker's performative act. The stanzas following the poem's several apostrophic passages suggest that apostrophe is deceptively solipsistic. Rather than transforming objects into subjects, apostrophe transforms the speaking subject into an object. For example, the stanza following the address to the waves begins:

> The young doctor is dancing with happiness
> in the sparkling wind, alone
> at the prow of the ferry.
>
> (*CP 1*, 102)

Although on its surface a celebration of lyric solitude, this passage re-places the lyric "I" with the more distanced, more objectified "young doctor," who proceeds to reject the present "curdy barnacles and bro-ken ice crusts" for a more nostalgic vision of this same landscape in summer. The next instance of apostrophe, this time addressed to "Long yellow rushes," has a much more alarming sequel:

> XII
> Long yellow rushes bending
> above the white snow patches;
> purple and gold ribbon
> of the distant wood:
> 　　　　what an angle
> you make with each other as
> you lie there in contemplation.
> 　　　　XIII
> Work hard all your young days
> and they'll find you too, some morning
> staring up under
> your chiffonier at its warped
> bass-wood bottom and your soul—
> out!
> —among the little sparrows
> behind the shutter.
> 　　　　XIV
> —and the flapping flags are at
> half mast for the dead admiral.
>
> (*CP 1*, 103)

The stanza following the personified "rushes" is itself apostrophic, but the voice is disembodied and sinister in its authoritative tone (the "you" addressed is not only the poet but a typical "you" that includes the reader). The sudden change of mood from the meditation on natural beauty to the admonition about death corresponds with the abrupt shift of address. As an objectified speech act, one whose speaker and ad-dressee cannot be determinately located, this stanza implicitly critiques the previous apostrophic passages. If the apostrophic act imbues the lyric speaker with the authority of poetic tradition—in this case the authority of the Whitman tradition—this authority itself is portrayed as a fiction. The fictional act of apostrophe is here associated not only with solipsism but with death. If lyric poetry exists only within the bounds of the fictional, of the aesthetic, of poetic tradition, if it has no social function in everyday life, then indeed the poet "alone / at the prow of the ferry" becomes the "dead admiral."

"January Morning" ultimately escapes the solipsism of postromantic lyric poetry by grounding the colloquy of speech acts within a conversation, a conversation elusively situated in the poet's locality:

> All this—
> was for you, old woman.
> I wanted to write a poem
> that you would understand.
> For what good is it to me
> if you can't understand it?
> But you got to try hard—
> But—
> Well, you know how
> the young girls run giggling
> on Park Avenue after dark
> when they ought to be home in bed?
> Well,
> that's the way it is with me somehow.
>
> (CP 1, 103–4)

This final address to "you, old woman" is frequently associated with Williams's paternal grandmother, Emily Dickinson Wellcome, but according to his recollections it was actually addressed to his mother, whose multilingual background and thwarted aspirations of becoming an artist played a formative role on Williams's literary identity throughout his career.[17] "January Morning" subtly situates Williams's construction of "national" literary descent within this "local" filiation. The poem's final reference to "Park Avenue" reiterates this double construction, as "Park Avenue," a main street of Rutherford, evokes the better-known Manhattan address. This reference bridges Whitman's New York with Williams's Rutherford, but it also establishes Williams's position for a "localist" avant-garde within the New York avant-garde. While acknowledging the difficulty of the poem's oblique juxtaposition of imagistic stanzas, the conclusion opens the process of interpreting the poem into a playful, rather than laborious, act. As an objective correlative for the poem's complex of feelings, the conclusion liberates the reader from the quest for symbolic correspondences, proposing instead a play of modes and images whose structure anticipates Williams's longer poetic sequences in the 1920s.

Williams more explicitly relates his emergence as a poet to his genealogical descent in "Dedication to a Plot of Ground." This poem narrates the life of Williams's "English" grandmother, his father's mother, Emily Dickinson Wellcome. The muse of Williams's important Keatsian long poem, "The Wanderer" (1914, but reprinted in *Al Que Quire!*), Emily Dickinson Wellcome was a subject Williams returned to throughout his career.[18] But although "Dedication for a Plot of Ground" is ostensibly a biography of Williams's grandmother, it actually tells us as much about his own "dedication" to a "plot of ground." The poem begins with a sentence broken into thirty-seven lines, most of them enjambed, that narrates the immigrant's journey to the "plot of ground" the speaker addresses. This opening sentence employs Whitman's paratactic catalog rhetoric, but with broken lines that enact a correspondence between fragmentary syntactic structures and the fragmentary experience of immigration. This long description of Wellcome's life follows, however, a simple declarative statement:

> This plot of ground
> facing the waters of this inlet
> is dedicated to the living presence of
> Emily Dickinson Wellcome.
>
> (*CP 1*, 105)

The "declaration" is immediately situated within a specific occasion honoring "Emily Dickinson Wellcome." However, the initial clause, although apparently identifying the poem's title as a ceremonial declarative act, raises contradictory interpretive possibilities that the poem never forecloses. The occasion for this dedication is not specified, as dedicating the "plot of ground" to the woman's "living presence" suggests that she may be neither living nor present. Is this "plot of ground" a burial plot for a woman whose "living presence" has endured beyond her death, or does this "living presence" describe someone indeed living and present, perhaps at the site of the dedication itself? If she is alive and present, then what does "living presence" oppose? By underlining, and undermining, the Christian implications of "living presence," the poem establishes a correspondence between belief in life after death and a state of death-in-life. This correspondence is especially ironic for a poem about a woman who converted to Christian Science late in her life. It is gruesomely ironic in that she developed skin cancer on her face after this conversion and refused medical treatment, even from her grandson. This act of de-facing the Christian "plot of ground," the "living presence" of Emily Dickinson Wellcome, raises further questions about the occasion of this dedication, rather than "grounding" the poem in a coherent linear "plot."

The title of the poem seems to describe the performative act of dedication, an act presumably addressed to an audience familiar with the poet's grandmother. Furthermore, the opening lines of the poem invert the subject and object of the acts described in the title. Rather than the poet's declarative act of dedication, the ground itself becomes the subject, "dedicated to the living presence . . ." As we find out by the poem's conclusion, the title also describes her "dedication" to this "plot of ground" she has settled, inhabited, worked, and defended:

> She grubbed this earth with her own hands,
> domineered over this grass plot,
> blackguarded her oldest son
> into buying it, lived here fifteen years,
> attained a final loneliness and—
>
> If you can bring nothing to this place
> but your carcass, keep out.
>
> (CP 1, 106)

Between the performative act of the title and the descriptive act of its conclusion, the poem reenacts the biography of the subject who has made the ground responsive to *her* performative act of dedication. But in foregrounding the peculiar fictionality of occasional poetry, in this case the speech act of dedicating the plot of ground, the poem foregrounds the fictionality of the kind of "plot" it surveys. The "plot of ground," like "Emily Dickinson Wellcome," marks a "living presence" that signifies an absence; the "ground" cannot be abstracted from the "plot" that defines it. The plot of ground as a piece of land, whether a garden "plot," a burial "plot," or simply a measured "plot" of property, cannot be apprehended apart from the graphic signification that differentiates it from any other "plot." Likewise, "Emily Dickinson Wellcome" cannot be divorced from the biographical "plot of ground" that these verses plow and the stanzas encompass. Positing neither a transcendent "ground" nor an exclusively self-reflexive "plot," "Dedication for a Plot of Ground" takes on a "living presence" only through the imaginative act of transforming the bare details of its biographical plot into a meaningful reconstruction of the immigrant American life it surveys. Its conclusion, like the title *Al Que Quire!*, acts simultaneously as an imagistic objectification of a speech act and a direct address to the reader. The poet's words here merge with those of his "living" grandmother, admonishing those who "bring nothing to this place / but your carcass" to "keep out," referring both to "this place" the poem dedicates and "this place" that is the poem.

"Dedication for a Plot of Ground" charts the chaotic, tumultuous course of Wellcome's journey to this "plot of ground"; it rehearses in a long Whitmanesque catalog an Odyssean life of repeated setbacks and subsequent recoveries. The "plot" of this heroic immigrant journey is narrated in two long sentences that report the events of her life in starkly simple clauses. The first sentence simply traces her descent from family to family, place to place, following the introductory clause, "who was born in England." The structure of the poem actually subverts the rhythm and the inclusiveness of the Whitmanesque line. By breaking the catalog of marriages, deaths, births, and catastrophes into short lines that frequently interrupt the syntax of the clauses, the poem accentuates the series of displacements that have defined Wellcome's life. The narrative "plot" of her life is characterized by two recurring features. The first is Wellcome's devotion to her children and grandchildren, even under the most difficult circumstances, such as the deaths of two husbands. The second is her ability to persevere and establish a home, to locate herself, wherever she found herself "aground." This narrative of the incredibly complex series of marriages, deaths, and births, and the equally complex series of journeys—from England to New York to the Caribbean and back to New York—presents her as a passive subject, specifically the subject of her husbands' decisions. The narrative shifts to the active voice only after her second husband's death, when she "followed / the oldest son to New York" and eventually "seized two boys of / the oldest son by the second marriage," i.e., when she simultaneously "grounded" herself in a specific place and enters the poet's consciousness.

Williams's act of tracing his grandmother's descent is of course an act of tracing his own descent. The "plot of ground" she eventually settled, "defended," "grubbed," and "domineered over" is the "plot of ground" construed from his memory of childhood summers. Yet the name of this figure through whom Williams constructs his genealogical descent may seem too coincidental for an American modernist poet, especially in a poem preoccupied with death and burial. And sure enough, Williams's grandmother was born "Emily Dickensen," according to his *Autobiography* (167), although orthographic consistency could hardly be expected for the name of a nineteenth-century immigrant. By replacing the *e* of Dickensen with *i*, Williams rewrites his genealogy to foster a direct line of poetic descent.[19] In "The American Background," Williams praises "the authenticity of Emily Dickinson's unrhymes" (*SE*, 155), but she nevertheless epitomizes the victim of Puritan repression he continually returns to in *In the American Grain*, "starving of passion in her father's garden" (*AG*, 179). Williams describes Dickinson's heroic but ultimately failed attempt to awaken from the narcotic "sleep" induced by American culture in his reflection on American women's writing in "The Somnambulists," a 1929 review of Kay Boyle's *Short Stories*:

> Awake, Emily Dickinson was torn apart by her passion; driven back to cover she imprisoned herself in her father's garden, the mark of the injury she deplored, an opacity beyond which she could not penetrate. And in literature, since it is of literature that I am writing, it is the mark of our imprisonment by sleep, the continuous mark, that in estimating the work of E.D., still our writers praise her rigidity of the sleep walker—the rapt gaze, the thought of Heaven—and ignore the structural warping of her lines, the rhymelessness, the distress marking the place at which she turned back. She was a beginning, a trembling at the edge of waking—and the terror it imposes. But she could not, and so it remains. (*I*, 340-41)

"Dedication for a Plot of Ground" releases her from her father's garden in the figure of Emily Dickinson Wellcome, who herself becomes an active subject in the poem only after the deaths of her husbands, after she writes a "plot" of her own. If "the passion, the independence and the determination of this woman born Emily Dickenson in Chichester, England" (*A* 167) represent those qualities Williams chooses to identify with his genealogical descent, by insisting on the *i* in "Dickinson" he simultaneously constructs a literary grandmother, whose structurally warped, rhymeless lines resemble Williams's "beginning" to compose in the "American idiom."[20] In conflating the "plot" of Williams's grandmother's life with the "plot" of reinventing that life, "Dedication for a Plot of Ground" rewrites the past to subvert any nativist "grounds" for constructing models of ethnic, national, or aesthetic purity.

Williams's most ambitious attempt before *Paterson* to position himself within a revised American literary past is of course *In the American Grain*. *In the American Grain* has enjoyed renewed prominence—especially in culturalist studies of American modernism—and illustrates most vividly how recent readings of Williams have actually been quite divided on how to reconcile his interpretation of American culture with his experimentation with poetic language and form. For example, in J. Hillis Miller's 1986 MLA presidential address, Williams meets the MLA not as a "token inclusion" in the academic canon of American literature, but as the author of a "great book about America," *In the American Grain*. In this address one of Williams's most influential academic critics takes up his interpretation of American history to forecast the future of literary studies, in the light of ongoing challenges to the canon's central position for defining the profession's identity, such as the increasingly multicultural, multilingual makeup of the American population, the ongoing impact of feminism, and the effect of socioeconomic and technological change on literacy. Citing Williams's "cultural critique" to address the "frontier" topic of current literary study in the United States—namely, the "question of the material base"—Miller argues that Williams's text supports his reading of the definitive characteristic of American culture, its "superficiality." Comparing Williams's interpretation of American culture to Nathaniel Hawthorne's and Henry James's, Miller argues that Williams "wants meaning or value to have the possibility of being not arbitrary, conventional, or simply positional but responsive to a potentiality for meaning that is already there, in the ground," but he ultimately "sees America . . . as the denial of this responsiveness."[21]

Miller's reading of *In the American Grain* typifies formalist readings of Williams that obscure the historicity of his linguistic and formal experimentation. By positing an Adamic site for reading, Miller simplifies *In the American Grain*'s self-conscious position in the literary tradition of the "American Adam."[22] Recent interpretations of *In the American Grain* as cultural criticism have in fact been quite divided, and they demonstrate that Williams's aestheticist, and at times even mystical, notion of the imagination's power to elevate experience from its contingent context often contradicts his historicist claims for representation. *In the American Grain* has been read as a text that exemplifies that "writing for Williams is *always writing history*," as its pluralistic juxtaposition of discursive practices foregrounds the materiality of language.[23] Conversely, it has been argued that *In the American Grain*, especially in its concluding chapter on Poe, rhetorically empties American history of "local" content to demonstrate the aesthetic imperative of antirepresentational modes of writing.[24] Thus, for Williams, "to liberate literature from reference, or representation, was to liberate its medium, words, from the associations and contexts of past usage—in short, history."[25] Although these arguments reach different conclusions, they all posit coherent, consistent versions of Williams's interpretation of history that encompass texts from different periods of his lifetime as well as from *In the American Grain*. But because of Williams's pragmatist approach to history, his interpretations of history must be located within their historical contexts. More specifically, in *In the American Grain* his interpretations of American history depend on the politics of national identity that inform Americanist literary canons.

As *In the American Grain* exemplifies, Williams did not subscribe to the influential romantic nationalism of Van Wyk Brooks or to Pound's, or especially Eliot's, expatriate inventions of Western culture.[26] As a sequence of imaginative portraits of selected New World historical figures and events, *In the American Grain* rejects the conventional narrative mode of national histories for a structure that has been compared to cubist collage or cinematic montage or, more recently, to the polyphonic novel. Even within individual chapters it spurns the expository mode of such contemporaneous revisionary accounts of American history as Brooks's *America's Coming of Age* (1915), Waldo Frank's *Our America* (1919), or D. H. Lawrence's *Studies in Classic American Literature* (1923). As a text that fractures historical perspective, rejecting realist modes of representation for reflexive modes of imaginative representation, *In the American Grain* complicates any assertions about its point of view as a "cultural critique." Most significantly, it carries out what Vera M. Kutzinski calls a "deconstructive revision" of "American" history, as it decenters canonical European and North American literary models, while challenging any unified version of American culture.[27] Its structure celebrates the diversity of the discoveries, explorations, and settlements of the Americas. As Bryce Conrad notes, *In the American Grain* is organized "like a debate between contending

cultural conceptions of what shape life in the New World should take,"
until this debate gives way to the dominant position the book counter-
poses, the Puritans'.[28] In juxtaposing perspectives both between and
within chapters—perspectives that are impressionistic or imagistic, "sub-
jectively" immersed in their topic or "objectively" detached—*In the
American Grain* simultaneously foregrounds the interpretive act of constructing historical narratives and the constructive act of interpretation.

The chapter in *In the American Grain* that most explicitly reflects
on Williams's Americanist avant-garde literary identity is "Père Sebastien
Rasles." A pivotal chapter for the book's autobiographical plot, "Père
Sebastien Rasles" is as concerned with Williams's self-definition as a
writer as it is with his definition of American nationality. This chapter
reconstructs the life of Rasles from his *Lettres édifiantes* within a dialogue between Williams and Valéry Larbaud, the French poet, novelist,
critic, historian of New World literature, and translator of Whitman
and Joyce's *Ulysses*. Before meeting Larbaud, Williams is uneasy about
his presumed intellectual inferiority to the Frenchman: "I could see it
at once: he knows far more of what is written of my world than I. But
he is a student while I am—the brutal thing itself" (*AG*, 107). This dialogue, which takes place in Larbaud's Paris apartment, concentrates more
on Williams's conception of Puritanism than on the life of Rasles, as
the two writers debate the more general issue of the differences between American and European cultures. Playing the primitive American "brutal thing," Williams's savage indictment of Puritanism leads to
Larbaud's characterization of him: "I see you brimming—you, yourself—with those three things of which you speak: a puritanical sense of
order, a practical mysticism as of the Jesuits, and the sum of those qualities defeated in the savage men of your country by the first two" (*AG*,
116). However convoluted his calculations are, Larbaud's analysis, or
psychoanalysis, of Williams's portrayal of colonial American history
aptly identifies the dividedness of Williams's self-presentation.

As a defense and demonstration of *In the American Grain*'s historiographic method, "Père Sebastien Rasles" contrasts Williams's diatribe
against the ongoing effects of Puritan thought with Larbaud's detached
analytic method of textual analysis. Williams persistently interjects his
disdain for Puritanism, personifying Mather in monstrous terms. As he
rants about the deleterious effects "the Puritans" have had on American culture, Larbaud repeatedly challenges his interpretations of Mather,
reminding him: "It is of books that we were speaking." If Larbaud, with

his "cultured tolerance," can find aesthetic beauty in Mather's writing, then Williams reads Mather as a source for the "ghostly miasm" that "has survived to us from the past" (*AG*, 115). Following Brooks, D. H. Lawrence, H. L. Mencken, and other contemporaneous critics of the "genteel tradition," Williams's "Puritanism" is a protean concept that can signify theological fundamentalism, aristocratic or theocratic politics, moral hypocrisy, sexual repression, censorship, and prohibition. Recasting American history as the Freudian conflict of will and body, repression and liberation, such arguments invert the conventional nationalist narratives of American history. The Indian emerges as the buried hero, while the Puritan and his avatars (the frontiersman, the businessman, the fundamentalist Christian) become the oppressive agents of an alien ideology imposed on the "American ground." Williams, however, situates Puritanism neither within an irreversible process of "the human condition to erase the material base"[29] nor as the only tradition of New World settlement. In addition to acting as a catachresis for the dominant commercialist ideology that makes twentieth-century America "immoral," "Puritanism" for Williams also exists within a contested field of texts that define New World history. By positioning his anti-Puritan polemic within "Père Sebastien Rasles," Williams decenters the Puritan tradition in New World history. Correspondingly he decenters his own Americanist perspective by incorporating this polemic within this dialogue with a skeptical French scholar of New World history.

Puritanism retains its ideological currency for Williams as a code for reading the relation of socioeconomic modernity to American nationalism. Defined primarily within the nationalist process of textualizing the New World "ground," "Puritanism" nonetheless has specific material consequences that align modernity with the Puritan past: "Americans have lost the sense, being made up as we are, that what we are has its origins in what *the nation* in the past has been; that there is a source in AMERICA for everything we think or do; that morals affect the food and food the bone, and that, in fine, we have no conception at all of what is meant by moral, since we recognize no ground our own— and that this rudeness rests all upon the unstudied character of our beginnings . . ." (*AG*, 109). In inscribing "Puritanism" within the terms accentuated by italics, "*the nation*," and by capital letters, "AMERICA," Williams foregrounds the ongoing material effects of nationalist discourse. Rewriting the past therefore not only becomes an act of recovering buried traditions, but an act of demystifying the terms of post–World

War I American nationalism. Without such critical study "of our beginnings," and without questioning the politics of reading the Puritan past as "our beginnings," Americans cannot "recognize" the "ground" they inhabit. Furthermore, Williams argues that "what has been morally, aesthetically worthwhile in America has rested upon a peculiar and discoverable ground" (*AG*, 109). By juxtaposing examples of such imaginative encounters with a "peculiar and discoverable ground," and by foregrounding the autobiographical process of discovering such texts, *In the American Grain* aims to provoke the re-cognition of the "ground" beneath the reader's "feet." In positing a ground that can neither be severed from nor identified with its national appellation, Williams stresses how textuality and materiality are interwoven. Precisely because the material "ground" cannot be apprehended in a primal, prehistorical encounter, the recognition of how material effects result from the textualization of this "ground" becomes a moral imperative for Williams. Those who ignore "what *the nation* in the past has been" unwittingly reenact the Puritan practice of typological reading, of seeing "one thing like another in a world destined for blossom only in 'Eternity'" (*AG*, 113). In doing so they reaffirm the structures of dominance that authorize and issue from this practice of reading, "blind to every contingency, mashing Indian, child and matron into one *safe* mold" (*AG*, 112).

In establishing a correspondence of the "ground" with "Indian, child and matron," Williams follows his "Puritans" in subsuming the differences of race, age and gender under the rubric of the natural or the primitive. But in critiquing the Puritan repression of the physical—collapsing the geographical ground with the body as ground—Williams locates the material effects of Puritanism in the racist and sexist practices authorized by the dominant "American" ideology. This same process of repressing the body (the "ground"), of reading the body as other, engenders the American practice of repressing the past. Williams's engagement with the texts of American history, both as material artifacts and as discursive practices with ongoing material effects, enacts his empathic identification with this protean "other." This process of identifying with the other is emblematized by the portrait of Rasles. However, Rasles is praised above all in negative terms, as an "anti-Puritan," the inverse of moral hypocrisy: "It is *this* to be *moral*; to be *positive*, to be peculiar, to be sure, generous, brave—to MARRY, to *touch* . . ." Because Rasles does not disdain "to MARRY, to touch" the New World "ground" or the Abenaki tribe he proselytizes, he is "released an Indian" (*AG*, 121). This "Indian" awaiting "release" characterizes the psychological condition of modernity in America: "Lost, . . . as in a forest, I do believe the average American to be an Indian, but an Indian robbed of his world—unless we call machines a forest in themselves." Collapsing the Puritan forest with the forest of machines, Williams situates his critique of Puritanism within a critique of modernity that mourns the displacement of authority from "the individual" and the "local government" to a government in which "everything is federalized and all laws become prohibitive in essence" (*AG*, 128). Williams's antifederalist response to modernity is nostalgically individualistic. Likewise his inversion of the Puritan/Indian opposition is hardly an adequate framework for critiquing a complex market economy. In positing the repressed "Indian" as the universal condition of the "average American," Williams reinscribes the discourse of American exceptionalism that his critique of Puritanism purportedly opposes. However, in refusing to read the Puritan/Indian opposition as *the* master narrative of New World history, *In the American Grain* subjects this opposition itself to interrogation. Because Williams's anti-Puritan polemic is located within the first-person narrative account of his dialogue with Larbaud, the "grounds" of his claims themselves become unstable.

Williams himself stresses the autobiographical importance of his research into American history, as he says to Larbaud:

> I speak only of sources. I wish only to disentangle the obscurities that oppress me, to track them to the root and to uproot them—
> Continue, he said. Adding, with a smile, You wish to uproot history, like those young men of the Sorbonne.
> No, I seek the support of history but I wish to understand it aright, to make it SHOW itself. (*AG*, 116)

Throughout *In the American Grain*, Williams reads history as a discourse of the unconscious, neither immediately decipherable nor entirely inaccessible. But he writes that the past must be confronted, and his historiographic method is itself analogous to Freudian psychoanalysis. As analyst of American culture, he interprets those texts repressed from the consciousness of his (American) readers, so that they will presumably recognize the "sources" of their ongoing conflicts. In representing the "source" of Puritanism through the chapter-long quotation of Mather's account of the witchcraft trials in *The Wonders of the Invisible*

World, Mather's archaic language itself symptomizes the neurosis which Dr. Williams sees afflicting American culture.[30] However, when Williams becomes the spokesman of American culture in the chapter following Mather's monologue, "Père Sebastien Rasles," his obsessive *anti*-Puritanism, his inversion of Mather's rhetoric, is read as a neurosis by *his* analyst, Larbaud.[31] As his anti-Puritan perspective is decentered within the dialogic encounter with Larbaud, Williams is positioned as both subject and object of the historiographic narrative. As analysand, he subverts his own historiographic authority as cultural psychoanalyst. Calling into question Williams's own enactment of the national character he critiques, "Père Sebastien Rasles" situates the quest for American "sources" in an international, intersubjective act of constructing the past. Rather than closing the inquiry with a conclusive act of authoritative judgment, "Père Sebastien Rasles" is ultimately an act that foregrounds the interpretive sites whereby readers rewrite the past. In going to France to "see a strange New World," Williams locates the American "ground" not in an ahistorical transcendent place of repeated discovery, but in a localized act of encountering what is "strange" and "new" in the "strange New World."

3

"To witness the words being born": Williams's Poetics of Dissent

Do we not see that we are inarticulate?
—William Carlos Williams, *Autobiography*

Probably Williams's best-known articulation of the symbiotic relation of his careers as physician and poet—namely, his *Autobiography* chapter entitled "The Practice"—immediately follows "Translations," in which he describes the liberating effect of translating from his "mother's native language as well as one which my father spoke from childhood" (*A*, 349). Because Spanish is not a "literary language" with the "classic mood of both French and Italian," translating Spanish literature allows one "to use our language with unlimited freshness . . . to branch off into a new diction, adapting new forms, even discovering new forms, in an attempt to find accurate equivalencies for the felicities of the past" (*A*, 349). To "see that we are inarticulate" implies an effort to articulate what we have not seen. To translate a language that resists English articulation requires an openness to unforeseen linguistic formations. Williams's diagnosis of the difficulties of translating Spanish literature into English recapitulates his prescriptions for American "avant-garde" poetry, poetry that deploys "new diction, new forms" not only to articulate what our impoverished linguistic habits prevent us from seeing but to see those forms through which we do struggle to articulate. Williams's characteristic fragmented syntax, with enjambed lines whose breaks defamiliarize grammatical relations and with rhythmic variations that aim to visually represent speech patterns, demands that we see how we are inarticulate. Similarly, his imagery of the body, of plant life (especially of flowers), and of liminal or marginal places foregrounds the physiological and ontological aspects of articulation. To "see that we are inarticulate" is both Williams's descriptive diagnosis of a social pathology and his prescriptive therapy for "discovering new forms," new forms with new diction that themselves engage readers to undergo this process of discovery, "to witness the words being born." Not just a heuristic metaphor, articulation operates as the dominant trope of Williams's poetics of dissent, both formally and thematically. It is not only the trope that connects "The Practice" to his poetic practice, but also the trope that connects and divides his poetics from succeeding practitioners in the "Williams tradition."

The impact of Williams's medical profession on his writing is usually treated in studies of his fiction or in studies of *Paterson*, where the epistemological and ethical dilemmas of the physician are more explicitly demarcated. His "doctor stories" best elucidate the often conflicting professional demands of the doctor as participant and as observer, but these conflicts inform the linguistic strategies of his lyric poetry as well.[1] In "The Practice," Williams describes how his medical practice provided him with the "basic terms" for his writing: "Was I not interested in man? There the thing was, right in front of me. I could touch it, smell it. It was myself, naked, just as it was, without a lie telling itself to me in its own terms" (*A*, 357). What preoccupies Williams is not so much the scientific challenge of diagnosing an illness but the hermeneutic challenge of comprehending the "terms" with which patients articulate their symptoms. As interpreter, Williams hardly maintains a detached perspective. In this instance, the shifting pronouns indicate that understanding the patient involves an empathic act of identification, if not an act of projection. The patient as representative "man" becomes the specific, objectified "thing," an "it" then transformed into "myself, naked." The process of interpreting the patient's "terms" of articulation in order to achieve a clearer, less deceptive self-understanding is elsewhere transposed to celebrate the physician's ability to "reveal a patient to himself." This sort of diagnosis, which Williams distinguishes from the "mere physical diagnosis" of patients, he equates with memorable writing: "And when one is able to reveal them to themselves, . . . they are always grateful as they are surprised that one can so have revealed the inner secrets of another's private motives. To do this is what makes a writer worth heeding: that somehow or other, whatever the source may be, he has gone to the base of the matter to lay it bare before us in terms which, try as we may, we cannot in the end escape" (A, 358). As interpreter of the "inner secrets" of the patient's "private motives," the writer is both reader and producer of the patient as text. The patient's articulation (of pain) compels the interpreter's diagnosis, while this diagnosis "reveals" the subtext(s) informing the patient's words. This exchange between patient and doctor becomes the model for exchange between the (literary) text and the reader/producer. In this analogy of the reader of the body as the reader of the literary text, the physician who witnesses the "words being born" is uniquely situated to foreground this very process of "words being born."

The physician's act of interpreting the patient's unconscious "private" motives is limited, if not obstructed, by the conventions of "public" discourse: "A thousand trivialities push themselves to the front, our lying habits of everyday speech and thought are foremost, telling us that *that* is what 'they' want to hear" (A, 359). But if the professionally coded constraints of doctor-patient discourse restrict the possibilities for productive dialogue, the "daily practice of medicine" nevertheless allows the doctor access to "that which the daily print misses or deliberately hides": "But day in and day out, when the inarticulate patient struggles to lay himself bare for you, or with nothing more than a boil on his back is so caught off balance that he reveals some secret twist of a whole community's way of thought, ... then we see, by this constant feeling for a meaning, from the unselected nature of the material, just as it comes in over the phone or at the office door, that there is no better way to get an intimation of what is going on in the world" (A, 359–60). Williams's trope of the doctor-patient exchange for the production of poetry is not centered on the patient attempting to express himself, nor on the words themselves. Rather it insists on the process of articulation, a process that includes both speaker and listener in the production of meaning. In order to understand how this dialogic process can spark an "intimation of what is going on in the world" the doctor must be fully receptive to the possible implications of the most mundane acts of articulation, to the "minutest variations" of "half-spoken words" (A, 362).

In "The Practice" such a state of receptivity is posed as an antidote to "our inability to communicate to another how we are locked within ourselves, unable to say the simplest thing of importance to one another" (A, 361). The struggle to communicate, to articulate what would otherwise remain unconscious, is figured as a process of giving birth:

"The physician enjoys a wonderful opportunity actually to witness the words being born. Their actual colors and shapes are laid before him carrying their tiny burdens which he is privileged to take into his care with their unspoiled newness. He may see the difficulty with which they have been born and what they are destined to do. No one else is present but the speaker and ourselves, we have been the words' very parents. Nothing is more moving" (*A*, 361). Not just the "witness" of the "words being born," the physician bears the responsibility to take them "into his care," not as a detached observer, but as a "parent." Yet the curious concluding reference to the patient and physician as "the speaker and ourselves" posits a proliferation of "parents" that separates the words from any fixed relation to either speaker or listener. The "speaker and ourselves" suggests a multiplicity of subject positions produced by the dialogic process of articulation, a process whose representation in writing conflates the physician interpreting the patient's words with the reader interpreting the physician's translations (of these words). Both the physician/translator and the reader are posited as "parents" to the words given birth by the patient; the reader is positioned as an active producer of meaning, a physician/translator of the transcribed words. The act of reading poetry thus requires the same attention to the process of articulation as does the act of listening to and diagnosing such "half-spoken words."

Williams's writings on the production and reception of poetry, especially during the 1920s, argue for a poetics that enacts such a process of witnessing "the words being born." The essays and notes that comprise *The Embodiment of Knowledge* explain the social function of such a poetics. One example Williams cites to demonstrate the significance of attention to the process of articulation is his own act of exteriorizing his "innermost convictions." The very act of struggling with language makes this process of articulation potentially threatening: "Afraid lest he be caught in a net of words, tripped up, bewildered and so defeated— thrown aside—a man hesitates to write down his innermost convictions" (*EK*, 104). If the expression of such convictions proves to be incoherent, "lost in a crashing together of words which will not be resolved into lucidity" (*EK*, 104), then one's "personal integrity" itself is threatened. However, such convictions are worthless if they cannot withstand the "test" of articulation: "For how can he be certain that his conviction, which if it be worth anything at all . . . is so, unless he test it explicitly by statement? It must be written down, bit by bit, as he may, in fear for his lack of skill at words, watching them, distrusting them—yet counting on them to help him, to bring what he knows he must believe into a searchlight of scrutiny. And who knows, it may be that he will succeed" (*EK*, 104–5). Such a process of self-articulation, of "testing" that which comprises one's "personal integrity," exemplifies the function of "literature" on a more complex social scale. In exposing and challenging how social life is "hedged round (officially) with its prohibitions, its fetishes, its don'ts, its bibles, commandments, rules of conduct, its 'laws'" (*EK*, 96), literature functions to "lead life from some modicum of bondage to fetishes and therefore stupidities" (*EK*, 97). By foregrounding the *process* of articulation, rather than a finished product, the literary text presumably avoids the fetishization it sets out to subvert.

Williams differentiates "the province of letters" from those intellectual fields that "use language as secondary to the reality of their own materials," but he does not argue for a purely aesthetic definition of art. Literature is defined by its function in relation to the functions of other fields of knowledge, its goal being "to re-enkindle language, to break it away from its enforcements, its prostitutions under all other categories" (*EK*, 20). By foregrounding words as the "material of letters" (*EK*, 18), through grammatical and syntactic play that defamiliarizes everyday usage, modern writers such as Joyce and Stein provoke the "mind's escape from the bondage to the past: there are no truths that can be fixed in language. It is by the breakup of the language that the truth can be seen to exist and that it becomes operative again" (*EK*, 19). Not escape from the past, but "escape from bondage to the past." Such "escape" implies a heightened recognition of the past, and thus a heightened recognition of historical difference. This enables a clearer comprehension of the transmission of linguistic structures to the present, while allowing for the possibility of revising such structures in response to present historical conditions. Poetry, because it foregrounds the process of articulation, produces knowledge that differs from that produced by science and philosophy: "[I]t is not the amount that a man knows but that he has achieved a clear vision through difficulties" (*EK*, 36). Nonetheless, poetry, like science, is successful insofar as it produces new knowledge, although such knowledge is hardly quantifiable: "[N]ew works must be based—or their criticism—on an increase of knowledge, and will be accepted or rejected solely upon that score. But it is their bodies as poems, as with men, that is their destiny, differing from all

writing which has not writing itself as its substance. . . . Or, if not the
increase of knowledge in an absolute sense, it may be the representation
of knowledge from an illegible script" (*EK*, 74–75). Williams vacillates in
locating the increase in knowledge produced by poetry: sometimes such
knowledge arises from the poet's subjective encounter with his material; sometimes the representation of the "illegible script" produces
knowledge in itself; and sometimes knowledge is produced purely by
the reader's encounter with the formal devices of the poetic text. What
these models for the production of knowledge share is their rejection
of aesthetic autonomy. Reading the poem as a "body" requires not only
a critical self-awareness of one's preconceptions as a reader but a willingness to actively participate in the production of knowledge.

The introductory poem of *Al Que Quire!*, "Sub Terra," epitomizes
how Williams's project of revising American literary history, i.e., his
poetics of descent, interacts with his simultaneously destructive and
creative experimentation with poetic form, or his poetics of dissent.
This poem, written in 1914, initially chides its readers; it issues its appeal to them as a challenge:

> Where shall I find you,
> you my grotesque fellows
> that I seek everywhere
> to make up my band?
> None, not one
> with the earthy tastes I require;
> the burrowing pride that rises
> subtly as on a bush in May.

(CP 1, 63)

The first word of this elevated appeal for "earthy tastes" is an appropriate beginning to a volume that is dedicated to grounding American poetry in the local. In asking "Where shall I find you," the poem mourns
the scarcity of readers receptive to Williams's aesthetic. But it also compels these readers to reflect on the specific place of their response, a
place differentiated from the poem's subterranean site of enunciation
but a place this initial rhetorical question charges with poetic possibility. The act of reading therefore becomes a process of re-cognizing the
"terra" from which this "Sub Terra" becomes meaningful. "Sub Terra"
does not sustain this initial aggressive challenge to its readers' taste. It
translates identification with the earth into a universal aesthetic principle,

the principle emblematized in the book's epigraph, translated by Williams as "an adventurous shrub which prolongs its filaments until it finds the necessary humus in new earth" (*CP 1*, 481). Looking beneath Whitman's *Leaves of Grass*, "Sub Terra" proceeds in a proto-stream-of-consciousness series of questioning, seeking, and positing sources for aesthetic satisfaction. It concludes by figuring this process with more imagistic formulations of the poet's subterranean vision. Williams's concluding "Sub Terra" imagery hardly evokes the imagist "rare world of H.D. and Ezra Pound,"[2] not even the underground world of "In a Station of the Metro":

> You to come with me
> poking into negro houses
> with their gloom and smell!
> in among children
> leaping around a dead dog!
> Mimicking
> onto the lawns of the rich!
> You!
> to go with me a-tip-toe,
> head down under heaven,
> nostrils lipping the wind!
>
> (*CP 1*, 64)

Wallace Stevens isolated the "Sub Terra" lines, "in among children / leaping around a dead dog," to exemplify what he thought most valuable in Williams's early poetry. "A book of that would feed the hungry," Stevens wrote in a letter Williams quoted in the prologue to *Kora in Hell* (*I*, 15). However, Stevens also notes his "distaste for miscellany" to criticize Williams's experimentation with "point of view": "Given a fixed point of view, realistic, imagistic or what you will, everything adjusts itself to that point of view; and the process of adjustment is a world in flux, as it should be for a poet. But to fidget with points of view leads always to new beginnings and incessant new beginnings lead to sterility" (ibid.). Stevens's critique applies to Williams's early poetry in general, but this multiplicity of perspective is adumbrated by the rhetorical shifts within "Sub Terra." The "I" in this poem ranges from the inclusive Whitmanesque epic perspective to the confrontational public mode of the "townspeople poems," to the realistic and imagistic modes of the nature lyrics, proletarian portraits, and urban pastorals, to the

mixed meditative, interrogative, and polemical modes of the self-portraits. These experiments with perspective, although often fragmentary
as Stevens claims, anticipate more fully developed poems in the 1920s
and later. For example, as didactic speeches addressed to his "townspeople," such poems as "Apology," "Foreign," "Riposte," "Gulls," and
"Tract" are often ignored by readers who situate Williams's early poetics exclusively within imagism, although this public mode of address is
dramatically employed in a later poem like "Impromptu: The Suckers."[3]
Conversely, the descriptive nature poems, meditations on such subjects as birds, flowers and trees, are more frequently acknowledged for
their prototypically kinesthetic presentation of the natural "world in
flux." The portraits of working-class subjects in *Al Que Quire!*, whether
a dramatic monologue like "Portrait of a Woman in Bed" or a descriptive poem like "Woman Walking," foreshadow Williams's "proletarian
portraits" of the 1930s. The most interesting poems of *Al Que Quire!*,
however, are not those that concentrate exclusively on the abstracted
community, the natural world, or isolated individuals, but those that
integrate such topics, combining public and private modes of address
into dialogic reflections on the purposes of and possibilities for poetic
statement.

The experimentation with point of view that Stevens criticizes can
be explained by the question raised in the opening line of "Apology":
"Why do I write today?" (*CP 1*, 70). By repeatedly asking "Why . . .
today?" the response to the ever-changing quotidian world does indeed
lead to "incessant new beginnings." However, there are recurring patterns to these new beginnings in Williams's early poetry. This same
question enables Williams to dramatize the relationship of the lyric "I"
to the poem's site of enunciation. Whereas the "I" is constituted by the
location of the poetic statement (a location defined generically as well
as by the place of its historical moment), this location is often transformed
by the imagistic "eye" reflecting on the objectified speaking "I." The
"urban pastoral" poems of *Al Que Quiere!*, for example "Pastoral" ("The
little sparrows") and "Pastoral" ("When I was younger"), perhaps best
exemplify the mind in the act of composing, the act of discovering novel
subjects and innovative rhetorical strategies for traditional lyric forms.
Unlike the direct, public modes of address in the townspeople poems,
Williams's urban pastorals are descriptive, reflective meditations on the
place of lyric poetry in the modern industrial world. Tracing the pastoral motif throughout Williams's career, Peter Schmidt has shown that

his pastoral poetry assumes the precisionist myth of America as a potential industrial arcadia.[4] Combining the traditional pastoral vision of rebirth with the Americanist rhetoric of discovery, Williams's urban pastorals follow the conventional pattern of comparing nature to artifice. More specifically, they explore the gap between pastoral ideals and modern American socioeconomic reality. Unlike the conventional pastoral, though, Williams's urban pastorals do not withdraw from ordinary life to an idealized natural setting. Rather, they situate the pastoral vision within the observed quotidian life of marginal urban figures. For example, "Pastoral" ("The little sparrows") affirms the act of quarreling:

> The little sparrows
> hop ingenuously
> about the pavement
> quarreling
> with sharp voices
> over those things
> that interest them.
> But we who are wiser
> shut ourselves in
> on either hand
> and no one knows
> whether we think good
> or evil.
>
> (CP 1, 70–71)

The personified sparrows do represent a typical pastoral construct, in this case representing the value of conversation, even in dispute, rather than the polite reserve of "those who are wiser." However, this poem situates this pastoral world on the urban "pavement," and the sparrow, a recurring figure of quotidian urban "nature" throughout Williams's poetry, represents a commonplace, mundane natural world. Furthermore, this poem concentrates less on constructing a pastoral ideal than on destroying the Christian conception of "pastoral":

> Meanwhile,
> the old man who goes about
> gathering dog-lime
> walks in the gutter
> without looking up
> and his tread
> is more majestic than

> that of the Episcopal minister
> approaching the pulpit
> of a Sunday.
>
> (CP 1, 71)

This comparison between the Episcopalian minister and the Wordsworthian lime-gatherer elevates the lime-gatherer's "tread" to a position "more majestic" than the minister's; it allies the lime-gatherer with
the first term of the initial comparison—with the sparrows on the pavement rather than with "we who are wiser." But in their solitude they are
both opposed to the quarreling sparrows. The old man in the gutter
actually grotesquely mirrors the man approaching the pulpit. Both are
products of the proud silence of "we who are wiser," a "we" with whom
the poet ironically identifies in the poem's conclusion:

> These things
> astonish me beyond words.
>
> (CP 1, 71)

James Breslin, among others, has argued that the conclusion of
"Pastoral"("The little sparrows") epitomizes Williams's early tendency
to moralize, to "proceed more from idea than from perception," even
when he is arguing for an "immediate encounter with things." The final
lines of "Pastoral" ("The little sparrows") in particular attempt to "cast
an aura of profound and mysterious significance over what has pro-
ceeded."[5] Breslin's critique typifies readings of Williams's early poetry
that base their evaluations on Pound's "list of don'ts." However, this
closing "enigmatic oracular utterance" not only violates imagist doctrine but critiques the ideology of romantic pastoral as well. This self-
reflexive statement wryly deconstructs the poem's binary system of
oppositions. "These things" has no specific reference; it signifies the act
of describing as much as the acts described, which are less "things" than
processes. And the "words" of this poem, by the very act of "quarreling," belie the literal reading of this closing statement. Because the poem
presents an open dialectic, its "closure" is more likely to produce further "quarreling" than silence. On the one hand, the closing statement
celebrates poetry's power to "astonish . . . beyond words." On the other
hand, this closing statement problematizes the poem's point of view.
Because the "we" initially contrasted to the quarreling sparrows includes
the poet, the poem implicates its speaker in the same stance of proud

superiority as the Episcopalian minister. The act of elevating the lime-gatherer to a position above the minister itself bespeaks the poet's priestlike authority; the act is condescending to the old man as it satirizes the minister. Situated in the primitive world first figured by the sparrows, the lime-gatherer becomes one of "these things." By suggesting that the celebration of the marginal lime-gatherer reifies its subject, turns him into a "thing . . . beyond words," "Pastoral" ("The little sparrows") questions the viability of the Wordsworthian pastoral vision for the modern industrial world. It asserts the power of "words" to make "things," or at least inscribe things with ideological significance, but this power can be dangerous. By suggesting that the poet's point of view is analogous to that of the Episcopalian "pastor," "Pastoral" ("The little sparrows") unveils the grounds of its own authority. Rather than an attempt to elevate the poem's subject matter to profound significance, its conclusion ironically undercuts such pretension. It reminds us that the relations of words to things cannot be fixed outside the act of enunciation.

The self-conscious process of objectification in "Pastoral" ("The little sparrows") is performed more complexly in "Pastoral" ("When I was younger"). This poem is frequently praised for its colloquial description of a decrepit urban scene, the "houses of the very poor":

> roof out of line with sides
> the yards cluttered
> with old chicken wire, ashes,
> furniture gone wrong;
> the fences and outhouses
> built of barrel-staves
> and parts of boxes, all,
> if I am fortunate,
> smeared a bluish green
> that properly weathered
> pleases me best
> of all colors.
>
> (CP 1, 64)

The line that stands out is the qualifying phrase, "if I am fortunate." Hardly a found object that the eye alights on, this chaotic cityscape is sought for its aesthetic quality. The rhetoric of discovery is revealed to be an artificial construct; the poet's "bluish green" smears the imagist object with his subjective presence. Even the choice of "barrel-staves" as building material reveals this artificiality, as *staves* implies poetic stanzas as well. What complicates this aestheticized cityscape is its frame. Like the previous pastoral poem, "Pastoral" ("When I was younger") questions its own function as a pastoral lyric.

"Pastoral" ("When I was younger") begins with a narrative comparing the poet's youth with his maturity:

> When I was younger
> it was plain to me
> I must make something of myself.
> Older now
> I walk back streets
> admiring the houses
> of the very poor.
>
> (CP 1, 64)

This initial sentence conceals the poem's reflexive structure within its cliché of the self-made man. The poet "makes something" of his observation of the urban slum in "plain" language. Although this observation is detached and objective ("admiring") in its precise descriptive language, it is willfully subjective in the self-conscious process of aestheticization. Transforming the "houses of the very poor" into a pastoral landscape, this poem is less ironic about this process of reification than "Pastoral" ("The little sparrows"). Instead, it celebrates its vision, concluding with a sardonic summary:

> No one
> will believe this
> of vast import to the nation.
>
> (CP 1, 65)

What was first a reflection on the poet's development becomes a "national" issue. As in the previous "Pastoral," this concluding statement contains a deictic indicator, "this," that can refer to both the descriptive act and the things described. Not only is the urban slum ignored by the "nation," but Williams's poetic treatment of such a topic presumably is ignored as well. The use of "import" accentuates this dual reference. In addition to suggesting "importance," *import* also suggests something imported. Williams's celebration of the urban slum implicitly celebrates the immigrants who inhabit this slum, however absent they are from the "houses" described in the poem. This celebration of immigrant bricolage celebrates the poem's own structure, itself "of vast import" not only to the national poetic tradition but to the pastoral tradition.

Williams's early poetry frequently invokes lyric traditions in the light of modern American social conditions that not only marginalize poetry but undermine the notion of a unified lyric "speaker." The book that most fully explores the difficulty of and necessity for interpreting and producing avant-garde art in American culture is *Spring and All*. *Spring and All*, like his other dadaist and cubist texts of the 1920s, is less concerned with Williams's "descent" as a writer than with his "dissent" not only from modern American commercialism but also from Euro-centric vanguardism. The most extensive analyses of *Spring and All* have concentrated on elucidating how its subversion of realist modes of representation borrows from and resembles European avant-garde movements in the literary and visual arts. Whether outlining Williams's affiliations with dadaism and cubism, or the interplay of both, analyses of *Spring and All*'s structure have stressed how its combination of various genres embodies avant-garde open-endedness, self-reflexiveness, multiplicity, and free play.[6] Not an autonomous, self-contained long poem or poetic sequence, the montage of genres that comprises *Spring and All* performs on a macroscopic scale what Jonathan Monroe attributes to the prose poem: "[A]esthetic conflicts between and among literary genres manifest themselves concisely and concretely as a displacement, projection and symbolic reenactment of more broadly based social struggles."[7] Although I am not specifically concerned with the structure of *Spring and All*, I would like to examine how the trope of articulation operates in what Perloff calls its "metonymic network" of images.[8]

Williams questions a variety of polarities in American culture in *Spring and All*: the poles of poetry and prose, poetry and painting, speech and writing, improvisation and craftsmanship, urban and rural, bourgeois and avant-garde. *Spring and All* deconstructs such polarities both in form and in theme. As a dialectic of poetry and prose, prose that is at times poetic, at times philosophical, at times polemical, and at times playful, it juxtaposes a variety of genres. And the individual poems themselves incorporate the generic instability of the sequence as a whole, as their prosaic language represents speech types and quotidian themes that Williams's contemporaries considered antipoetic. Most importantly, *Spring and All* is structured like a personal journal or diary, foregrounding the discontinuities of everyday life amid the continuities of natural change ("spring and all") and the acts of improvisation amid the demands to reconstruct experience into socially acceptable aesthetic forms. *Spring and All* questions the politics of genre; it is critical and self-critical in its manifestations of the limits of generic definitions. It is especially critical of the lyric tradition and its privileging of the isolated, supposedly ahistorical subject. And in its concern with quotidian language and themes, it questions the politics of generic structures that exclude working-class and other marginal speech types, as well as "domestic" subject matter normally considered feminine. *Spring and All* does express a nostalgia for unmediated presence; in fact, its rhetoric and form enact a continual process of discovery, a process analogous to the New World discovery narratives Williams draws from in *In the American Grain*. Yet this process undermines the notion of an Adamic lyric "I"; *Spring and All* compels its readers to see "a new world naked," but its rhetoric and form compel us to consider the subject positions from which we read this world.

The famous opening poem of *Spring and All*, later titled "Spring and All,"[9] epitomizes the physician's vision as poet's vision, while exemplifying the themes and techniques Williams explores throughout the book. The opening line of "Spring and All," "By the road to the contagious hospital" (*CP 1*, 183), places the poem in a medical context. The adjective *contagious* suggests that the hospital is itself contagious, that it does not contain disease, that sickness is an ever-present state in this bleak landscape. The entire book, as well as this poem itself, can be seen as Williams's response to Eliot's depiction of the modern world as a wasteland. But it should also be seen as Williams's response to the wasteland world of poverty and disease he knew as a doctor. Williams's rendering of his wasteland of clouds, cold, mud, and dead plants gives it a stark beauty, however. The "purplish, forked, upstanding, twiggy / stuff of bushes and small trees" (*CP 1*, 183) stands not as thematic background but as something worth examining in itself. The poem's lineation compels us to notice the singularities and connections of these roadside images. There is no punctuation at the ends of lines, and the syntactic sense often precludes an expected end stop. For example, in the lines "under the surge of the blue / mottled clouds driven from the / northeast" (*CP 1*, 183), "blue" and "mottled" are separated by the line break, yet they are semantically fused. The eye jumps from what is normally an adjective, "blue," to the next line to find the noun, "clouds," but the line break suggests that "the blue" is itself an entity. The lineation produces the effect of a windy spring sky, the "blue mottled clouds" changing so rapidly that we must pay close attention to distinguish "blue" from "clouds." Similarly, the lines "purplish, forked, upstanding, twiggy / stuff of bushes and small trees" (*CP 1*, 183) achieve this sense of dynamic process. These adjectives are separated by commas, and although they all modify "stuff," they evoke individual plants before jumping from "twiggy" to "stuff of bushes and small trees." The effect is one of constant shifts in perspective, from the clouds to the fields to patterns of landscape to details of the roadside growth—all portrayed without grammatical connectives. This process of vision and revision resembles the doctor's openness to his patients' attempts to articulate their symptoms. Like the patient, the landscape is approached and examined "naked, just as it was, without a lie, telling itself . . . in its own terms" (*A*, 357).

Williams's thematic retort to Eliot's more pessimistic vision occurs later in the poem; when in Williams's landscape spring arrives, life is renewed:

> They enter the new world naked
> cold, uncertain of all
> save that they enter. All about them
> the cold, familiar wind.
>
> (*CP 1*, 183)

"They," following the approach of "sluggish dazed spring," evokes the shoots growing from the earth, but the syntax leaves the referent of "they" ambivalent, suggesting a more general concept of birth, physical rebirth that is spiritual in the sense of absolute faith in rebirth, "uncertain of all / save that they enter." The wind is "familiar," not shocking, to the newborn simply because there are no preconceptions in plant life, or in newborn life in general: the newborn adapt to environmental conditions that become immediately "familiar" because there is no sense of otherness. The late winter wasteland will give birth to spring whether we interpret it or not; the child will struggle to survive whether it is cared for or not.

The conclusion of "Spring and All" reiterates Williams's physician's vision of examining the world empirically, rather than symbolically: "One by one, objects are defined— / It quickens: clarity, outline of leaf" (*CP 1*, 183). These lines epitomize Williams's rejection of "crude symbolism" in *Spring and All*: "The word must be put down for itself,

not as a symbol of nature but a part, cognizant of the whole—aware—
civilized" (CP 1, 189). The "clarity, outline of leaf" represents not only
the "leaf" of spring growth but the page as "outline of leaf" as well, the
frame that directs our attention to the "clarity" of vision the words
evoke. Hugh Kenner incisively summarizes Williams's poetic vision in
terms that are also applicable to the doctor's vision: "This ability to
move close to quite simple words, both hearing them as spoken—not
quite the same thing as hearing their sounds—and seeing them interact
on a typewritten page, gives Williams the sense of constant discovery.
. . . 'No ideas but in things' meant that the energy moving from word to
word would be like that of the eye moving from thing to thing, and not
like that of the predicating faculty with its opinions."[10] The closing imagery of "Spring and All" articulates the doctor's and the poet's "sense
of constant discovery" in the figure of birth as rebirth. The newborn are
"rooted," as they "grip down" through their roots and "begin to awaken."
From the decay of winter arises the rebirth of spring growth; from the
poverty of northern New Jersey arises the will to survive. Although
death and decay are ever-present, the promise of new life and rebirth
never disappears. There are no sentimental notions about spring here,
only a belief in the indomitable will to be born, to survive.

The figure of birth that closes "Spring and All" typifies Williams's
insistence throughout Spring and All for new forms and new language
to return poetry to everyday life. The book begins with a characteristi-
cally avant-garde gesture, an overtly antagonistic challenge to its readers: "If anything of moment results—so much the better. And so much
the more likely will it be that no one will want to see it" (CP 1, 177).
Not only a "sour grapes" reflection on critical reactions to Williams's
previous books, this introductory statement redefines the colloquial-
ism "anything of moment" into an epistemological, ethical, aesthetic
imperative to counteract the "constant barrier between the reader and
his consciousness of immediate contact with the world" (ibid.).
Williams's project in Spring and All entails not so much establishing
this "contact" as exposing and subverting poetic strategies that divert
the imagination from any "articulation" of its immediate world. This
simultaneously destructive and creative project requires a productive
reader whom Williams defines in dialogic, intersubjective terms: "When-
ever I say, 'I,' I mean also, 'you'" (CP 1, 178). Only writing that produces
such an author/reader relationship can engage the reader's imagination.
Such work "rouses rather than stupefies the intelligence by demonstrating

the importance of personality, by showing the individual, depressed before it, that his life is valuable—when completed by the imagination." The example for engaging the reader's imagination that Williams most often cites is Juan Gris's cubist collages, in which "the attempt is being made to separate things of the imagination from life, and obviously, by using the forms common to experience so as not to frighten the on-looker away but to invite him" (CP 1, 194). As studies of Williams's cubist technique in Spring and All have noted, his close attention to the "articulation" of part to whole, in form and in content, in poems such as "The Pot of Flowers" and "The Rose" demonstrates his literary ad-aptation of Gris's method for animating still lifes.

The challenge for the poet to use "the forms common to experi-ence" is that he must translate the "common thing which is *anonymously* about us" (emphasis mine) (CP 1, 189).[11] One strategy Spring and All posits for the poet to name the anonymous, to articulate the unarticu-lated, is the strategy of "rediscovery," a strategy personified in the vi-sion of the "farmer and the fisherman," whose need to accurately read the natural world gives them "residual contact between life and the imagi-nation which is essential to freedom" (CP 1, 187). This reliance on the natural world impels them to "rediscover or replace demoded meanings to the religious terms," words that are "demoded, not because the es-sential vitality which begot them is laid waste . . . but because meanings have been lost through laziness or changes in the form of existence which have let words empty" (CP 1, 187–88). Spring and All is full of primitivist figures whose contact with the natural world gives them more immediate access to the primal "meaning" of words, from the "com-posing /—antagonist" figure of "The Farmer" (CP 1, 186) to the "black eyed susan" of the concluding poem, whose "savage" features synop-size the book's most affirmative recurring imagery (CP 1, 236). Such primitivist imagery, which assumes a more direct physical contact within language between the subject and her world, does not predominate throughout Spring and All, however. As David Frail explains, the book is structured as an ambivalent dialogue between the (New York) urban world and the suburban pastoral world, in which the pastoral realm of imagination represents both withdrawal and engagement, sharpening the conflict between poetry and modernity.[12] The conservative mode of "rediscovery," of articulating a purportedly truer relation between words and things, is overshadowed by the more direct engagement with mo-dernity, specifically with linguistic change.

Williams's most obvious strategy for presenting the process of articulation is his representation of speech acts, whether as dramatic monologues or embedded within more descriptive forms. There are a number of poems that foreground the impact of modernity on oral discourse, not just to demonstrate alienation from language but to personify acts of struggling with such inarticulateness. For example, "To an Old Jaundiced Woman" describes a patient in grotesque imagery, but the patient nevertheless retains the desperate dignity of the subjects of his later "proletarian portraits." Her mouth is portrayed as the site of disease; however, she manages to utter a statement whose repetition starkly dramatizes how her condition emblematizes the "universal in the particular": "I can't die / I can't die" (CP 1, 215–16). The process of articulation is similarly counterposed to death in the opening dialogue of "Death the Barber." But if the barber's comparison of death to sleep—"he said, we die / every night" (CP 1, 212)—can diminish the fear of knife to throat, the poem's representation of oral discourse eternalizes the speech act while reifying its dynamic qualities. This problem of reification is even more evident in the dramatic monologue "Shoot it Jimmy!," which represents the African American urban vernacular of its speaker. The closing assertion of this poem is problematized by the transcription of the speech act:

> I make 'em crazy
>
> with my harmonies—
> Shoot it Jimmy
>
> Nobody
> Nobody else
>
> but me—
> They can't copy it.
>
> (CP 1, 216)

"Shoot it Jimmy" subtly deconstructs its own pretensions to "witness the words being born," to transcribe oral discourse "originally" without depleting its vitality. Even though the short syncopated lines evoke the rhythms of jazz, the "copy" of oral discourse indeed does accentuate the difference between speech and writing. The act of writing is never an "original" act of naming but is always an act of copying.[13] Yet

these examples of represented speech are themselves instructive, as "To
Have Done Nothing" perhaps best demonstrates. The playful experimentation with the minute grammatical variations of its title, when ac-
tivated by the "diphthong / ae," demonstrates how an "infinity of /
combinations" arise from the multiple social codes through which the
speech act takes place (*CP 1*, 191–92). So much depends on the sensitivity and openness to the linguistic configurations of social change.

Social change is hardly uniformly affirmed in *Spring and All*. In poems that concern such mass cultural spectacles as the movies ("Light
Becomes Darkness") or the baseball game ("At the Ball-game"), the
destructive aspects of modernity are stressed. Similarly, "Rapid Transit," a poem that mixes modes of address and the discourses of journal-
ism, advertising, and social welfare campaigns, begins by sarcastically
questioning poetry's ability to produce knowledge relevant to modern
social conditions:

> Somebody dies every four minutes
> in New York State—
>
> To hell with you and your poetry—
> You will rot and be blown
> through the next solar system
> with the rest of the gases—
>
> What the hell do you know about it?

(*CP 1*, 231–32)

Nonetheless, the destructive sense of speed evoked by the juxtaposed
metropolitan discourses of "Rapid Transit" cannot be simply left behind for the advertised

> Acres and acres of green grass
> wonderful shade trees, rippling brooks
>
> Take the Pelham Bay Park Branch
> of the Lexington Ave. (East Side)
> Line and you are there in a few
> minutes
>
> Interborough Rapid Transit Co.

(*CP 1*, 232)

The predominant mode of confronting social change in *Spring and All* is to incorporate the "rapid transit" of shifting images and discourses into the poems' processes of articulation, so that the effects of social change can be witnessed in "the words being born." One strategy for figuring this process is to situate the poem within the perspective of the poet as automobile driver. Williams of course spent much of his time in his car, making house calls, driving to and from the "contagious hospital," using this solitude and the rhythm of driving to compose verses. The cubist technique of a poem like "Spring and All," for example, can be seen as a mimesis of driving; the speed, the stop-and-go rhythms, and the sudden glimpses of roadside objects are evoked in a dynamic structure of rapidly shifting perspectives.

Several poems in *Spring and All* defamiliarize quotidian imagery through the driver's perspective. Perhaps the most obvious, most playful example is in "The Right of Way":

> In passing with my mind
> on nothing in the world
>
> but the right of way
> I enjoy on the road by
>
> virtue of the law . . .
>
>   (*CP 1*, 205)

The driver describes his glimpses of several memorable personages: "an elderly man," "a woman in blue," and "a boy of eight." "In passing with my mind" fuses spatial and temporal perception, with the sense of passing as going forward or past "nothing," or the sense of "passing" the time on "nothing." There is initially nothing disturbing in this "passing"; the driver is in a relaxed, hypnotic state until he asks:

> Why bother where I went?
> for I went spinning on the
>
> four wheels of my car
> along the wet road until
>
> I saw a girl with one leg
> over the rail of a balcony.
>
>   (*CP 1*, 206)

There is no punctuation here to guide the reader. Is this girl one-legged? Or does she have one of her two legs over the rail of the balcony? Or if she is one-legged, is that one leg "over the rail of a balcony"? Or is this one-legged girl over the rail? The immediate reaction to such a "suspended" ending is to reread the previous stanzas, to reconsider the "supreme importance / of this nameless spectacle." But these previous stanzas offer no conclusive answers to relieve the ambiguity of the poem's closure. "The Right of Way" is followed with this statement: "When in the condition of imaginative suspense only will the writing have reality, as explained partially in what precedes" (ibid.). Such "suspense," such ambiguity, operates unconsciously, compelling us to reflect on images that have flickered past too quickly to have been consciously considered. But as in the ambivalent, yet violent conclusion of "The Young Housewife" (*CP 1*, 57), where the doctor-poet's voyeuristic perspective is equally problematic, ignorance of such unconscious impulses impelled by the "rapid transit" of modernity is potentially deadly.

The most famous poem in *Spring and All* that presents the automobile as a figure of modern American mobility is "To Elsie." In this case, the automobile has no driver, and mobility is portrayed as mindless, aimless nomadism. "To Elsie" dramatically thematizes the trope of articulation to fuse Williams's revisionary poetics of descent with his avant-garde poetics of dissent. More than any Williams poem other than *Paterson*, "To Elsie" has drawn praise as a formally complex act of social criticism. Louis Zukofsky singled out "To Elsie" in his overview of 1920s American poetry, asserting that it brilliantly demonstrates the "social determinism of American suburbs in the first thirty years of the twentieth century." "To Elsie" exemplifies for Zukofsky that "history is in these pages and in the poems—history defined as the facts about us, their chronological enlivening for the present set down as art as so good for the next age and the next."[14] More recently, the cultural anthropologist James Clifford has read "To Elsie" as an exemplary text of "ethnographic modernity." Williams's standpoint of participant observation in "to Elsie" is ethnographic in that he "finds himself off center among scattered traditions," while modernity is encountered through the poem's complex evocation of lost authenticity.[15] Unlike the patients who are presented with medical-aesthetic distance in other Williams poems, the emblematic figure of "Elsie" is a "troubling insider" within the doctor-poet's bourgeois domestic space.[16] As Clifford argues, "Elsie" embodies not just a figure of modernity but a "plurality of emergent

subjects" whose representation resists any facile symbolic interpretation.[17] Elsie embodies the interpretive problem of the poem: unable to
articulate any notion of "contact" with her locale, the poem "strains" to
articulate the signs of her inarticulateness. David Frail argues that "To
Elsie" successfully diagnoses the failure of modern American culture
by demonstrating the gap between social reality and the terms by which
the "poet of contact" criticizes it. In other words, the poem succeeds
through its recognition of Williams's failure as a poet to restore the
promise of American culture.[18] I agree that "To Elsie" acknowledges
this problematic gap between the pathology of modernity and the poet's
prescription of contact, but the act of articulating this gap itself contradicts the poem's bleak conclusion.

Like "Spring and All," "To Elsie" depicts northern New Jersey as a
desolate wasteland of the "pure products of America," with its "deaf-
mutes, thieves,"

> old names
> and promiscuity between
>
> devil-may-care men who have taken
> to railroading
> out of sheer lust of adventure—
>
> and young slatterns, bathed
> in filth
> from Monday to Saturday
>
> to be tricked out that night
> with gauds
> from imaginations which have no
>
> peasant traditions to give them
> character.

(CP 1, 217)

From its oxymoronic opening of purity produced through this catalog
of aimless and inbred grotesques, "To Elsie" vitriolically indicts a
commercialist American culture that substitutes "gauds" for the local
gods of "peasant traditions." The possibility for a poetics of "contact"
to counteract such a desperate condition of rootlessness does indeed
seem to be a delusion. The inarticulateness that results from the lack of
any meaningful connection to place is personified in "some Elsie," whose

name itself suggests both alienation from the place she inhabits and otherness from the poet's perspective. The "broken / brain" with which she expresses "the truth about us" is suggested by the poem's syntax of one long sequence of progressive subordination, each phrase stated as a present apprehension, "broken" into short lines that frequently stop, unpredictably, to interrupt clauses, creating an effect of reckless speed combined with wandering, incomplete thoughts.

However, if "To Elsie" replicates the psychological effects of the social conditions it critiques, its articulation of its subject's inarticulateness suggests that poetry's close attention to language, whether on the level of the utterance or of the word, still serves the vital social function of producing knowledge. The diction of "To Elsie" is vaguer than in Williams's more descriptive poems. The description of the "pure products of America" is characterized by clichéd social types who appear to be "pure" because of their ideologically produced naturalness. Elsie, despite the oblique description of her as "voluptuous water / expressing with broken / brain the truth about us" (CP 1, 218), is largely an amalgam of sociological and physiological clichés. However, such vague colloquial diction is not consistent throughout the poem. Most notably, the description of plants is remarkably precise, as exemplified in the Saturday night scenario of the "young slatterns" succumbing without

> emotion
> save numbed terror
>
> under some hedge of choke-cherry
> or viburnum—
> which they cannot express—.
>
> (CP 1, 217)

The specificity of "choke-cherry /or viburnum" is accentuated by the vagueness of "some hedge." Furthermore, this inability to express, to name, is dramatized by the very selection of trees under which they "succumb." The "choke-cherry" is a North American wild cherry tree with astringent fruit, hence its name, while the "viburnum" is a member of the honeysuckle family whose Latin meaning is "wayfaring tree." The names of the trees thus figure both the "numbed terror . . . which they cannot express" and the nomadism of the "devil-may-care men." The only other plant named in "To Elsie" similarly suggests the psychological, even physiological, effects of the inability to express:

> while the imagination strains
> after deer
> going by fields of goldenrod in
>
> the stifling heat of September
> Somehow
> it seems to destroy us
>
> It is only in isolate flecks that
> something
> is given off
>
> No one
> to witness
> and adjust, no one to drive the car.
>
> (CP 1, 218–19)

"Goldenrod" is commonly confused with ragweed as an allergenic plant. Such common ignorance would surely discourage the "imagination" from pursuing "deer / going by fields of goldenrod." This ignorance is the result not so much of the inability to articulate a sense of "contact" with the local, but rather of the inability, or refusal, to reflect on the linguistic "grounds" for articulating such contact.

"To Elsie" foregrounds the significance of language not just in the "isolate flecks . . . given off" by its precise naming of plants but in its mixture of discourses that initiates reflection on the social roots and effects of clichéd terms and phrases. The poem certainly demonstrates and defends the poet's social function of naming. The phrase "the imagination strains" itself suggests a physical act of hunting, "strain" being derived from the Latin *stringere*, to "draw tight," as a bow, which "gives off" the "isolate flecks," evoking the French for "arrow," *flèche*. However, to "strain after" such a self-reflexive meaning is not the "point" of "To Elsie." Like its syntax, its patterns of sound accentuate the significance of close attention to everyday language, whether through alliteration or through the repetition of larger semantic units like "isolate . . . desolate . . . isolate." The "isolate flecks" of precise description not only reveal the poet's ability to name: they highlight the reader's responsibility for interpreting and transforming the quotidian terms which evoke our inability to articulate social relations. The poem's final stanza expresses the despair of modernity in the figure of a driverless car, but "no one / to witness / and adjust" can also be read against the colloquial grain as "no *one*/ to witness / and adjust." If the poet relinquishes the role of the "one" who drives the car, "To Elsie" acknowledges its readers' productive role "to witness / and adjust," to not only "witness the words being born" but to adjust the terms by which such words are conventionally understood.

4

"Pure Products": Imitation, Affiliation, and the Politics of Female Creativity in Denise Levertov's Poetry

Your idiom, Bill, is so unique that no one following you can approach it without danger—it's high tension wire.
—James Laughlin, letter to William Carlos Williams

We look at imitation askance; but like the shell which the hermit-crab selects for itself, it has value—the avowed humility, and "the protection."
—Marianne Moore, "Archaically New"

"High tension wire" and "the shell which the hermit crab selects": these figures for poetic imitation could hardly be more dissimilar. James Laughlin's characterization of Williams assumes that his distinctive "idiom" generates a profound anxiety of influence, an anxiety he himself had experienced both as poet and editor. Williams's idiom, according to Laughlin, is characterized by the intonation and cadence produced by his manipulation of the poetic line, specifically by the way his line breaks defy syntactic expectations.[1] Any poets who appropriate such formal devices do so at their own risk. Laughlin argues that those who have been most successful at adapting Williams's energy without succumbing to the "high tension wire" of his idiom—namely, Denise Levertov and Robert Creeley—share his "simplicity of statement," his elliptical style, and his use of American speech, but are original in "imposing their own sound patterns on the framework."[2] To write unlike Williams is therefore to write like Williams, to shape spoken language into distinc-

74

tive patterns, to formally indicate that one's poetry "speaks" differently from one's predecessors, not only because one's voice is "unique" but because spoken language most clearly registers the impact of linguistic change. So why does Williams's idiom produce so much "tension" for those who adopt his poetics? And furthermore, why, as Marianne Moore asks, do we look at "imitation askance"? Is the desire to supersede one's "influences" the primary motivation for post-Enlightenment poets, as Walter Jackson Bate and Harold Bloom have so influentially argued?[3] If not, then does such an understanding of Western literary history reflect a masculinist bias that privileges the individual over the community, patterns of individuation over patterns of connection? How *can* one value the "avowed humility" demonstrated in imitation?

Such questions about "originality" and "influence" that Laughlin and Moore raise are complicated further when the imitating writer is a woman, and complicated yet further when she is a postmodernist writer imitating an avant-garde writer who values formal innovation so highly. In their feminist revision of Harold Bloom's Freudian model of literary influence, Sandra Gilbert and Susan Gubar argue that twentieth-century women writers have shared a distinctive "female affiliation complex." Contrary to models of literary production based predominantly on either authorship or influence, Gilbert and Gubar assert that "affiliation" represents both choice and continuity, choice of literary descent and continuity of tradition through this choice. Such a choice, however, does not preclude an anxiety of influence that is experienced even more acutely by women. Adapting Freud's terms for female sexuality, Gilbert and Gubar explain that a woman writer has three options for finding a place in literary tradition: the normative renunciation of desire for the literary mother in order to accept the tradition of the father, the rejection of both allegiances to extricate herself from her own literary ambitions, or the deviant claim of the maternal tradition as her own.[4] They argue, however, that Freud's model is insufficient for describing twentieth-century women's visions of autonomous female creativity and of a matrilineal heritage that represents maturity rather than regression.[5] Gilbert and Gubar's model of modernism, which views avant-garde literary forms largely as a reaction to the rise of popular women's writing, is similarly insufficient for describing women poets who write in experimental, open forms. Their model of modernism, based primarily on the high modernism of Eliot and Pound, is especially problematic for explaining why Levertov joined so many postwar poets in choosing

Williams, who is not included in Bloom's pantheon of "strong poets," as the "shell the hermit-crab selects for itself." This chapter examines how Levertov's imitations of Williams perform an act of affiliation with an avant-gardist male predecessor without renouncing a vision of autonomous female creativity. Her imitations of Williams—notable for their very lack of anxiety—neither simply accept nor reject this literary "father." Instead, Levertov produces a feminized version of Williams distinctive from other more masculinist versions of him constructed in the "poetry wars" of the 1950s and 1960s.

In 1944, after repeated rejections by publishers who blamed the wartime shortage of paper, Williams published a volume of poems he had first conceived as *The Lang(WEDGE)*, then simplified to *The Language*, before finally settling on a military metaphor for his title, *The Wedge*.[6] Williams's introduction to this collection marks an important reevaluation of the social function of poetry, and more specifically, of the objectivist poetry he was producing during such a time of crisis:

> The war is the first and only thing in the world today.
> The arts generally are not, nor is this writing a diversion from that for relief, a turning away. It *is* the war or part of it, merely a different sector of the field. (*CP* 2, 53)

At about the time Williams was assembling the poems that would comprise *The Wedge*, Levertov was addressing "the war" from a much closer vantage point in her first published poem, "Listening to Distant Guns." With its regular iambic meter, its assonance, consonance, and rhymes, and with its gently ironic evocation of a pastoral world only mildly shook by the "low pulsation" of "distant guns," Levertov's poem is even more distant from "the war" that Williams conceives.[7] Although not a "diversion" from the war "for relief," "Listening to Distant Guns" hardly answers Williams's conviction that "there is no poetry of distinction without formal invention. . . . Such war, as the arts live and breathe by, is continuous" (*CP* 2, 55). Williams's introduction to *The Wedge* represents a crucial point of reference for postwar avant-garde poets. Levertov, however, working as a civilian nurse in London while writing the melancholy, meditative poems of *The Double Image* (1946), poems whose style associated her with the "New British Romanticism," had not yet enlisted in Williams's "continuous war" of poetic forms. Not until she married an American writer, Mitchell Goodman, and moved to Paris, was she introduced to Williams's work (first *In the American*

Grain and then his poetry). And not until she subsequently emigrated to the United States was she able to "hear" the poet whose American speech rhythms were until then alien to her ear. She describes the transformation of her poetics that resulted from this immersion in Williams's writing with the conviction of religious conversion: "Williams showed me the way, made me listen, made me begin to appreciate the vivid and figurative language sometimes heard from ordinary present-day people, and the fact that even when vocabulary was impoverished there was some energy to be found in the here and now."[8]

Williams's impact on Levertov's poetics is most evident in her poetry of the 1950s, collected in the first two books she published in the United States, *Here and Now* (1957) and *Overland to the Islands* (1958).[9] Levertov's most notable tributes to her mentor are those poems that incorporate not only Williams's technical devices, but his characteristic themes as well. A poem like "Pure Products," for example," appropriates not only the stance of the empathetic observer in "To Elsie" but also Williams's presentation of typically pathetic Americans divorced from any "contact" with their environment. Levertov's representation of a group of elderly "pure products" abroad in Mexico,[10] however, executes a subtle revision of Williams's stance, as her poem celebrates the empathetic nature of his social criticism while questioning the corresponding tendency to objectify his subjects. The poem begins with a humorous description of the American tourists:

> To the sea they came—
> 2000 miles in an old bus
> fitted with brittle shelves and makeshift beds
> and cluttered with U.S. canned goods
> > —to the Sea!
> on which they paddle
> innertubes   —and the lowhovering Sun!
> from which the old woman hides her head
> under what looks like
> a straw wastebasket.
>
> > (*CEP*, 76)

These absurd descendants of "Elsie" are portrayed in terms that stress the disorder of their assemblage, the "brittle shelves and makeshift beds," the bus "cluttered" with canned goods, the woman wearing a hat that "looks like / a straw wastebasket," but Levertov's tone is considerably less bitter than Williams's, suggesting a more tolerant appreciation of the

improvisational spirit of such accoutrements. The following stanza, however, represents the "pure products" in more grotesque, more pitiful
terms:

> "Yep, they cured me all right,
> but see, it made my breasts grow like a woman's."
> And she: "Something hurts him in his chest,
> I think
>   maybe it's his heart,"—and hers
> I can see beating at the withered throat.
>
> (*CEP*, 76–77)

This dialogue could easily be a quote from one of Williams's doctor
stories. Such an obvious imitation of Williams's stance suggests that
these grotesques emblematize Levertov's own self-conscious relation
to Williams's poetics; she is the "pure product" who makes use of whatever is at hand to fashion her own poem, even if it resembles a "straw
wastebasket" in comparison to his poetry. The conclusion of the poem,
however, dramatizes Levertov's simultaneous act of empathizing with
and distancing herself from Williams's vision:

> They are dying
> in their gentleness, adorned
> with wrinkled apple smiles—nothing
> remains for them
> but to live a little, invoking
> the old powers.
>
> (*CEP*, 77)

The absence of anger distinguishes Levertov's "pure products" from
Williams's; she leaves behind the impulse to ridicule and to blame that
drives "To Elsie." Instead she compassionately recognizes the sorry
plight of having nothing left but to "live a little." The final line does pay
homage to her mentor, though, as "Pure Products" acknowledges that
it has invoked "the old powers" of his writing; the poem accentuates
the empathetic side of Williams's vision by its own remarkable stance
of humility.

Of all the New American Poets, Levertov is probably most frequently identified with Williams's poetics. Her imitations of Williams's
form and diction, as in "Pure Products," have been criticized for their
unusual lack of anxiety of influence. James Breslin, for example, has

compared Levertov favorably to contemporaries like Charles Olson and Allen Ginsberg in noting that she makes no exaggerated claims of accomplishing an absolute break with the past, but this "modesty" makes her "less ambitious in proportion as she is less pretentious."[11] Most of Levertov's readers have commented on the similarity of her stance to Williams's poetic stance of the empathetic observer, her similar attention to the concrete, physical, quotidian world, and her similar use of spoken language, even if her diction differs from his "American idiom."[12] However, the specifically objectivist stance of the introduction to *The Wedge* is crucial for understanding Levertov's difference from Williams and his Black Mountain advocates. She formulates her open form stance largely in response to the Black Mountain interpreters of Williams's poetics, most notably Creeley, whose poetics are especially informed by his reading of the objectivist poets. Williams's objectivist credo refashions the theory of imitation through imagination he had formulated as far back as *Kora in Hell* and *Spring and All*. He argues that through a grasping of particulars, and a subsequent objectification of these carefully observed particulars, the poet can create an art object that enacts a human realization of natural creative forces, an art object that is itself an open, dynamic process rather than a closed, static product. Charles Olson's theory of projective verse reiterates Williams's—and of course Pound's—arguments for open-form poetics, while explaining the technical means for accomplishing such a dynamic process: the notion of the line as breath-spaced and the use of the printed page as the means for scoring the poem for speech. Yet what differentiates Williams from Pound similarly differentiates Levertov from her Black Mountain contemporaries. It is a difference that Pound himself often noted about Williams: the ability of the "foreigner" to objectify American speech. Adopting Williams's stance of the empathetic observer while immersing herself in his poetry, Levertov's imitations of Williams's objectify his characteristic idiom, thus enacting a postmodernist intertextual revision of Williams's poetics that questions the modernist privileging of technical innovation.

Most critics have agreed that even Levertov's 1950s poems that most resemble Williams reveal a greater emphasis on the poet's emotional, psychic involvement with her subject matter than on the "things themselves." Her 1960s accentuation of the spiritual quality of such "ecstacy [sic] of attention" subsequently clarifies, or intensifies, the quotidian experience presented in this early poetry. As in Williams's poetry, there is a continuum of living space and aesthetic space, of her life as a housewife/ mother and as a poet. But those who have noted Levertov's differences from Williams stress how her experience as a woman colors the world she reads; they say her poetry of domestic life is marked by a distinctively feminine consciousness of personal, private, circumscribed experience. Levertov has attracted considerable attention from feminist critics, not because her poetry is overtly feminist in its political stance but because she has frequently written on topics specific to her experience as a woman. She herself has stated that women's poetry is not a "special literary category."[13] Criticizing women poets who use poetry to "'express themselves' or to propagandize with little or no comprehension of what poetry, the art and mystery, in fact is," Levertov argues that the creative mind transcends gender, although without reducing it to neutrality. She appeals to men and women alike to "develop a sensibility more androgynous," a sensibility of "humane comprehension of the perceptive and receptive being in balance."[14] Many critics comment on how such a balance is accomplished through the continuity of her domestic experience with her immanentist poetics of the quotidian. Sandra Gilbert, for example, concludes that although Levertov is not "aggressively feminist," her poetry of "revolutionary love" is predominantly concerned with the materiality of her life as a woman.[15] Domestic experience becomes sacred in Levertov's work, especially through the emblematic presentation of domestic space as physical and spiritual shelter. Although a psychic doubleness that splits the observing artist from the nurturing wife/mother is prevalent in Levertov's work, the realization that the two roles can never absolutely coincide is represented as a liberating, rather than painful, experience, according to Gilbert. Other feminist critics have stressed how such poems as "A Woman," "The Earthwoman and the Waterwoman," "Sunday Afternoon," "Rose White and Rose Red," "An Embroidery," and "In Mind" dramatize the experience of the woman poet struggling with and against a divided self, experienced both as inescapable and intolerable.[16] Rachel Blau DuPlessis argues most convincingly that such conflicts between nurturing others and self-absorption, between marriage and pilgrimage, are informed by a belief in resolution, but the temporary resolutions frequently prove to be unstable. Comparing Levertov to Adrienne Rich and Muriel Rukeyser, DuPlessis emphasizes how Levertov's recurring theme of creation and re-creation of the self is performed through poetic epiphanies of self-discovery. Like Rich and Rukeyser, Levertov contributes to the invention of a reevaluative quest myth that reveals and critiques patterns that uphold traditional consciousness of women. Through her enactment of personal awakening to political and social life, through the historical specificity of her quest for self, Levertov criticizes the timeless, ahistorical pattern that informs traditional quest myths.[17]

DuPlessis's analysis of feminist revisions of quest myths is especially important for understanding how Levertov transforms Williams's poetics. Levertov has explained her poetic development as an exploration of ways to unite the "spirit of here-and-now that I had learned from Williams . . . with the romantic spirit of quest, of longing to wander toward other worlds."[18] She has addressed the significance of Williams's poetics for her own practice on numerous occasions. The 1970 essay "Great Possessions" is probably her most cogent summary of Williams's impact on her writing. In it she compares her poetry to the modifications of his poetics by other postwar poets. Distinguishing her practice of "magic realism" from what she calls the "Midwestern Common Style" of "documentary realism," she argues that those who cite Williams as a proponent of "documentary realism" misunderstand his theory of the imagination. The "notation poems" that result from this misunderstanding merely report things seen or done, without the "focus of that energetic, compassionate, questioning spirit that infused even the most fragmentary of Williams's poems." It is not sufficient to merely tell what one has seen without conveying a sense of "the experiencing of seeing or doing, or of the *value* of such experience."[19] Emphasizing Williams's insistence on the power of the imagination to conceive newness in the world, Levertov adopts one of his metaphors for this imaginative act to summarize her own aims for writing: "We must have an art that translates, conveys us to the heaven of that deepest reality which otherwise we may die without ever having known; that *transmits* us there, not in the sense of bringing information to the receiver but of putting the receiver in the place of the event—alive."[20] Such acts of translating experience into language, of conceiving "the heavens and hells that lie about us in all seemingly ordinary objects and experiences," do not simply heighten our perception of everyday life.[21] These imaginative acts are revolutionary, she argues, in showing "the vagueness and slackness of ninety percent of our lives."[22] Levertov's translation of Williams's poetics of the quotidian, the literary practice of "magic realism" she advocates in "Great Possessions," is thus not only a practice of seeing, but a political practice of questioning, of understanding what is ideologically constructed as natural, and ultimately of defying commercialist trivializations and reifications of everyday experience.

"Great Possessions" describes a synthesis of the "here and now" of Williams's poetics with the pilgrim's spirit of quest that Levertov's readers have generally found missing from her poetry before *With Eyes at the Back of Our Heads* (1961). It is commonly assumed that her earliest open-form poems imitate Williams's formal and rhetorical strategies too closely to be considered anything but successful "apprentice" work. Levertov herself has written that the poetry collected in *Here and Now* and *Overland to the Islands* quite consciously imitated Williams's characteristic vision, diction, and lineation. However, I would like to examine how these early poems do not simply appropriate Williams's poetics of the quotidian but adopt his dualistic stance of "descent" and "dissent" heuristically, to question the place of poetry in everyday life. Like Williams, Levertov blends reflections on her ancestral past with constructions of her literary "descent." In "Illustrious Ancestors," for example, she traces the lines of her descent from her father's Hasidic Jewish ancestry ("The Rav / of Northern White Russia" who "prayed / with the bench and the floor") and from her mother's Welsh ancestry ("Angel Jones of Mold, whose meditations / were sewn into coats and britches") (*CEP*, 77). These "illustrious ancestors" foreshadow her choice of poetic "lines":

> Well, I would like to make,
> thinking some line still taut between me and them,
> poems direct as what the birds said,
> hard as a floor, sound as a bench,
> mysterious as the silence when the tailor
> would pause with his needle in the air.

> (*CEP*, 78)

Similarly, she reflects on the distance from her British childhood to her adult American life in "A Map of the Western Part of the County of Essex in England":

> Something forgotten for twenty years: though my fathers
> and mothers came from Cordova and Vitepsk and Caernarvon,
> and though I am a citizen of the United States and less a

stranger here than anywhere else, perhaps,
I am Essex-born.

(P, 21)

This poem concludes by bridging the memory of herself as the child "who traced voyages / indelibly all over the atlas" (P, 22) with the collective experience of New World immigrants, whose compulsion to imaginatively experience their world is necessarily more pragmatic:

> All the Ivans dreaming of their villages
> all the Marias dreaming of their walled cities
> picking up fragments of New World slowly,
> not knowing how to put them together nor how to join
> image with image.

(P, 22)

This imaginative meditation on her childhood concludes with a vision of beginnings, of open possibility, but this vision of origins significantly arises from a representation, the map, of her childhood landscape. This vision of "the first river, the first / field, bricks and lumber dumped in it ready for building" (P, 22) celebrates the intertextual process of her "exploratory" mode of open-form poetics.

Levertov, like Williams, explains her eschewal of closed forms in terms of both mimesis and poesis. Closed forms imply a stable world of certainty and thus have "less relation to the relativistic sense of life which unavoidably prevails in the late twentieth century than modes that are more exploratory, more open-ended."[23] Such "exploratory" poetry "incorporates and reveals the *process* of thinking/feeling," which although not exploring experience in a way that is "wholly new" can nonetheless be "valuable in its subtle difference or approach: valuable both as human testimony and aesthetic experience."[24] This process of concurrently representing and formulating experience, the "energetic, compassionate, questioning spirit" she admires in Williams's writing, of presenting the mind in the act of perception, or "exploration," compels her dialogue with Williams's poetics in her 1950s poetry.

Not all of Levertov's poetic responses to Williams are as deferential as "Pure Products." One poem that addresses Williams's practice quite directly in order to express her dissent from his stance is the title poem to *Overland to the Islands*. Like many of Levertov's 1950s poems, "Overland to the Islands" meditates on the process of creation while in the act of creating. This poem in fact both asserts and demonstrates a practice that subverts the aesthetic principles that inform Williams's tightly structured imagist and objectivist poems. "Overland to the Islands" begins with a direct statement of Levertov's practice: "Let's go—much as that dog goes, / intently haphazard" (*CEP*, 55). The poem then describes the dog as an aesthetic object and demonstrates the "intently haphazard" process of attention that the stanza's concluding lines reassert:

> The
> Mexican light on a day that
> "smells like autumn in Connecticut"
> makes iris ripples on his
> black gleaming fur—and that too
> is as one would desire—a radiance
> consorting with the dance.
>
> (*CEP*, 55)

The images in this description are primarily painterly in evoking the play of light and color, but the quotation "'smells like autumn in Connecticut'" disrupts any notion that "intently haphazard" description is purely notational. This quotation interiorizes the act of perception and foregrounds the intertextual, linguistic bases of seeing. "Intently haphazard" description is a "dance" of subject and object, mind and world, imagination and perception, as the poem's concluding portrait of the dog as open-form poet affirms:

> Under his feet
> rocks and mud, his imagination, sniffing,
> engaged in its perceptions—dancing
> edgeways, there's nothing
> the dog disdains in its way,
> nevertheless he
> keeps moving, changing
> pace and approach but
> not direction—"every step an arrival."
>
> (*CEP*, 55)

Williams similarly demonstrated his formal strategies through the figure of the dog, most notably in *Paterson* but in several shorter poems as well. One such poem from Williams's 1948 collection *The Clouds*, "The Banner Bearer," is especially germane to "Overland to the Islands":

In the rain, the lonesome
dog idiosyn-
cratically, with each
quadribeat, throws

out the left fore-
foot beyond
the right intent, in
his stride,

on some obscure
insistence—from bridge-
going
into new territory.

                                              (*CP* 2, 137)

In both poems, the poet assumes the stance of the empathetic observer; each represented dog is an "intent" projection of the poet. But Williams's "lonesome" dog is portrayed more objectively by a more distant observer, while "that dog" in Levertov's poem is presented more empathetically. Her dog is not imbued with the aura of mystery that animates Williams's "idiosyncratic" dog, acting on "some obscure / insistence." "Overland to the Islands" displays no compulsion to define the dog's "intent." Levertov also renounces Williams's unified point of view, presenting the dog first as an aesthetic object and then in the act of moving. Rather than focusing intently on the singular moment, capturing the dog in the act of walking, Levertov dramatizes the process of perception, of understanding the significance of the moment. Rather than concentrating solely on the physical action of walking, Levertov foregrounds the dog's interaction with the world. This poem is not tightly sculpted into a series of brief broken lines as Williams's is; Levertov's lines retain the kinesthetic effect of Williams's poem with their inconclusive end words and lack of ending punctuation, but her lines, too, appear "haphazard" in their irregular rhythms and varied lengths. Rather than the intent progression of the "Banner Bearer" toward "new territory," we have the haphazard dog "dancing edgeways . . . moving, changing / pace and approach but / not direction—'every step an arrival.'"

The concluding quotation to "Overland to the Islands" further qualifies Levertov's appropriation of Williams's technique. This quotation is taken from a letter Rilke wrote upon returning to Paris after World War I, a letter that describes how after "those terrible years," he is able to feel again "the continuity of his life": "[A]part from political muddle and pother, everything has remained great, everything strives, surges, glows, shimmers—October days—you know them. . . . *One* hour here, the first, would have been enough. And yet I have had hundreds, days, nights,—and each step was an arrival."[25] If Williams's "banner bearer" is a distinctively militaristic figure for the avant-gardist compulsion to move ever forward into "new territory," then Levertov's "intently haphazard" dog figures a subtle revision of such an aesthetic program that privileges technical progress. "Overland to the Islands" takes from Rilke a complementary impulse to internalize, or "insee," this experience. Levertov cites Rilke's explanation of "inseeing" in another letter whose illustrative example is obviously relevant to "Overland to the Islands":

> Can you imagine with me how glorious it is to insee, for example, a dog as one passes by—insee (I don't mean in-spect, which is only a kind of human gymnastic, by means of which one immediately comes out again on the other side of the dog, regarding it merely, so to speak, as a window upon the humanity lying behind it—not that)—to let oneself precisely into the dog's very center, the point where it begins to be a dog, the place in it where God, as it were, would have sat down for a moment when the dog was finished, in order to watch it under the influence of its first embarrassments and inspirations, and know that it was good, that nothing was lacking, that it could not have been better made . . .[26]

The "aesthetic ethics" that Levertov learned from Rilke, "the attitude towards one's work that must underlie style and craft,"[27] compels such an "intently haphazard" movement that reverently accepts what one's "imagination" discovers, whether "rocks and mud" or scraps of Williams and Rilke. Rilke's distinction between "inseeing" and "in-specting" informs Levertov's revision of Williams's poetics. To "travel overland to the islands"—as the poem's paradoxical title announces—requires such a commitment to the imaginative process of "inseeing," of experiencing the interaction of art with everyday life, that the process of "moving, changing" itself becomes the experience of "every step an arrival."

"Overland to the Islands" rewrites Williams's objectivist aesthetic through a self-conscious, but playful, process of exploring how different rhetorical stances alter modes of perception, and correspondingly, how different modes of perception alter relations of subject and object. Although its self-reflexive form revises such a stance as Williams's in "The Banner Bearer," its intertextual reference to his canine figure for the avant-garde simultaneously celebrates the example of his technique. For Levertov, the avant-gardist compulsion to move toward "new territory" of technical accomplishment is left behind for a strategy of appropriating and recombining prior forms, a strategy that is both humble in its deference to earlier writers and defiant in its renunciation of "originality" as the poet's primary aim. Such appropriation of others' words is not entirely satisfying, as "The Rights" states quite directly:

> I want to give you
> something I've made
>
> some words on a page—as if
> to say "Here are some blue beads"
>
> or "Here's a bright red leaf I found on
> the sidewalk" (because
>
> to find is to choose, and choice
> is made).   But it's difficult:
>
> so far I've found
> nothing but the wish to give. Or
>
> copies of old words? Cheap
> and cruel; also senseless.
>
> (*CEP*, 32)

"The Rights" affirms "the wish to give" as meaningful in itself, but the questions this poem raises about representation and creation, mimesis and poesis, reverberate throughout Levertov's early poetry. For example, "At the Edge" raises the possibility for an absolute correspondence between poem and world:

> How much I should like to begin
> a poem with And—presupposing
> the hardest said—
> the moss cleared off the stone,
> the letters plain.
>
> (*CEP*, 115)

"And" presumes that the poem is already written, waiting to be transcribed, but such a perfect poem is a cold, inanimate object. The second stanza admits that such an aim for poetry settles for "apocrypha" rather than "true revelation," and thus forecloses the possibility for discovery:

> That poem indeed
> may not be carved there, may lie
> —the quick of mystery—
> in animal eyes gazing
> from the thicket,
> a creature of unknown size,
> fierce, terrified, having teeth or
> no defense, but whom
> no And may approach suddenly.
>
> (*CEP*, 115)

To "begin / a poem with And," to complacently presume one's mastery over the unknown, closes one's mind to whatever may appear at "the edge" of consciousness, erasing otherness by the presupposition of sameness. Such a prejudiced approach captures the unknown experience only by reifying it.

A number of Levertov's early poems, like "Overland to the Islands," explore the process of discovering poetic material in everyday experience. However, the process of discovery is more frequently presented as an act of questioning how different modes of representation "translate" what one sees. For example, the initial poem of *Here and Now*, "The Gypsy's Window," plays an instructive role comparable to its counterpart in *Overland to the Islands*. This poem begins with an impression of "the gypsy's window" that initiates a dialectic of observation and speculation:

> It seems a stage
> backed by imaginations of velvet,
> cotton, satin, loops and stripes—.
>
> (*CEP*, 29)

By beginning with "It seems a stage," the poem dramatizes the observer's act of imagining the life behind the window, of reading a world through its revealing details. "Imaginations of velvet" reiterates this appeal, although here, "imagination" is not exclusively located within either the scene composed by "the gypsy" or the scene composed by the poet's selection of details. The second stanza further dramatizes this reciprocal process of observation and speculation:

> A lovely unconcern
> scattered the trivial plates, the rosaries
> and centered
> a narrownecked dark vase,
> unopened yellow and pink
> paper roses, a luxury of open red
> paper roses—.
>
> (*CEP*, 29)

The adjectives describing the scene display the poet's will to discover, or posit, a design for the "scattered" gathering of objects, even if the attributed motivation for this design, a "lovely unconcern," is as unconscious as the movement of the "haphazard" dog. The "paper roses" accentuate this dual process of mimesis and poesis; as paper representations of roses themselves, they are as fictive as the poet's representations of them. The role of the imagination for interpreting the roses' significance, or for making them significant, is further impressed in the following stanza:

> Watching the trucks go by, from stiff chairs
> behind the window show, an old
> bandanna'd brutal dignified
> woman, a young beautiful woman
> her mouth a huge contemptuous rose—.
>
> (*CEP*, 29)

This passage defamiliarizes the symbol of the rose, mixing contempt with its more conventional connotations of romantic love. This "contemptuous rose" affirms the poet's power to defy conventional expectations, to appropriate a clichéd symbol, and furthermore a modernist trope *for* the clichéd symbol, for innovative purposes. Or, like the subject of her poem with her paper roses, the poet makes something vital out of an otherwise grim, constricted life of "stiff" chairs, of a "narrownecked" vase and "unopened" roses.

The final stanza of "The Gypsy's Window" renews the dialectic of observation and speculation, returning to the less-assertive mode of exploration with which the poem begins:

> The courage
> of natural rhetoric tosses to dusty
> Hudson St. the chance of poetry, a chance

> poetry gives passion to the roses,
> the roses in the gypsy's window in a blue
> vase, look real, as unreal
> as real roses.
>
> (CEP, 29)

The apparent oxymoron of "natural rhetoric" epitomizes the synthesis of observation and speculation that this fragmentary passage evokes. The "chance of poetry" is a "chance / poetry," a poetry of found objects, but found objects imbued with significance by the "passion" with which they have been arranged, both by the "gypsy" and her mirror image, the "gypsy" poet. This concluding stanza mixes terms of intention and arbitrariness. "Natural rhetoric" requires "courage," but to "toss ... the chance of poetry" is hardly an assertive intentional act. "Chance" itself is conventionally something that happens without discernible human intention or observable cause; it is the result of impersonal, purposeless activity. But the act of observing, of reading a world through a collection of found objects, opposes such a passive stance. The "courage" that "tosses to dusty / Hudson St. the chance of poetry" makes its own "chance." The tentative terms for this act suggest that it is an act of hubris, but an act that nonetheless affirms the "passion" of imaginative observation, that sees a "blue / vase" where earlier had been a "narrownecked dark vase."

Both "The Gypsy's Window" and "Overland to the Islands" dramatize how the poet "chances" on her material and, in the process of representing that material, imaginatively transforms it. Each of these poems is meditative, yet assertive of its aesthetic and ethical principles. A number of Levertov's 1950s poems, especially those that record the dramatic contrasts of life in Mexico, are less reflective, more resolute in their lines of questioning the poet's interaction with her material. "The Whirlwind," for example, posits a place for poetry both profound and desperate:

> The doors keep rattling—I
> stick poems between their teeth to
> stop them.
>
> (CEP, 79)

Poetry here apparently serves as a means of protection, a means for keeping the violent world of the "whirlwind" outside. However, although the "rattling" is caused by the stormy weather, it is actually the doors themselves the poet attempts to silence. The poem proceeds to describe in vivid detail the whirling movement of the "brown dust" outside her window:

> The brown dust
> twirls up outside the window, off
> the dead jicama field, scares the curtains,
> spirals to the dirty hollow
> where the cesspools are, and the most ants,
> and beyond—to the unfenced pasture land, where nothing
> will get in its way for miles and it
> can curtsey itself at last into
> some arroyo.
>
> *(CEP*, 79–80)

From behind the protection of door and window, the "dead," "dirty," "unfenced" landscape can be admired as a sublimely desolate stage for the playful "twirl," "spiral," and finally, "curtsey" of the "brown dust." Yet when the dust dances beyond the poet's sight, the rattling doors once again overwhelm her consciousness:

> The doors
> keep rattling—I'm
> shivering, desperate for a poem
> to stuff into their maws that will
> silence them. I know what they want:
> they want
> in all their wooden strength
> to fly off on the whirlwind into
> the great nothingness.
>
> *(CEP*, 80)

Only by immersing herself within the violent power of the natural world, the world of the unconscious as well as the "outside" world, only by acknowledging that not only the doors are illusory protection, but also the source of her anxiety, can her poetry incorporate, rather than silence, their rattling.

"The Whirlwind," like "The Gypsy's Window," questions what—the door, the window—precludes immediate apprehension of the world. Although it affirms the aesthetic need to release one's conscious control over perception, to submit oneself to the world in all its cacophonous, treacherous chaos, it does not pretend that such release enables the subject's total immersion into the world of experience. Only through subjection to the mediated process of perceiving the world can such immersion be approximated. "The Palm Tree" similarly questions whether the conscious act of seeking "the poetic" can be anything but an act of reifying what one has sought. Like "The Whirlwind," it depicts a world transformed by storm, a world whose frenzy the poem rushes to replicate:

> How the mule-eared palm, half paralyzed
> has quickened overnight! Scraping
> leaves beating!
>   (strained flags . . .)
> The palm tree in frenzy!

(CEP, 55)

The series of exclamation points signifies the poet's inability to convey such a charged world, as the following passage indicates:

> At once the mind, agape,
>   scavenging:
>
> What's human here? what hope is here?
> thumbing the dry leaves
> eager, eager, for the fabulous
> poem there may be
> in this delight or battle
> day coming and the moon not gone.

(CEP, 56)

Only by accepting this inability to represent the landscape transformed by the destructive storm, and by translating this frustration into a dramatic presentation of the mind "scavenging" for expression, does the poet draw a correspondence between poem and world. The poem goes on to enact this correspondence between the trees "Scraping / leaves beating" and the poet's "thumbing the dry leaves":

> And all morning the palm tree
> thick trunk immobile
>   abandons
>   its awkward leaves
>   (all its life awake

in struggling leaves . . .)
And only after the wind
is quenched
the tree dull
a quietness come
does the scraping mind perceive
what is possible
there are no miracles but facts.
To see! (there might be work
a challenge, a poem)

The squat palm!

(*CEP*, 56)

The poet's tumultuous quest for "miracles" is abandoned for the acceptance of "facts." "The Palm Tree" inverts the process of "At the Edge"; instead of the rejection of a mimetic model of poetry for the receptiveness to the "quick of mystery," here we have the countermovement toward the simple affirmation of the "squat palm." A resolution is reached through the echo of Williams's "To a Solitary Disciple," with its repeated command to "observe," to "grasp," to "see" (*CP 1*, 104–5). The act of simply asserting a "fact," the "squat palm," a fact reverberating with its intertextual allusion, is a humble recognition that the storm the poem tries to replicate is both overwhelming in its force *and* mundane. The exclaimed "fact" is itself an act of internalizing the storm's mundane power; the exclamation point accentuating the simple observation affirms the poet's act of naming, an act that affirms the power of its intertext while nonetheless celebrating the "scavenging" process that leads to its concluding discovery. In both cases, however, the process of exploring the mind's unpredictable movement toward clarity makes the final resolution, however tentative or contingent, significant.

"Beyond the End" is the poem that perhaps best demonstrates how Levertov's open-form strategy for questioning not only how one "chances" on poetic material, but how one's mode of representation transforms this material. This poem begins by comparing the forms spontaneously generated through "natural" energy to those imposed by human will:

In "nature" there's no choice—
flowers
swing their heads in the wind, sun & moon

> are as they are. But we seem
> almost to have it (not just
>   available death)
>
> It's energy; a spider's thread: not to
> "go on living" but to quicken, to activate: extend.
>
> (*CEP*, 30)

The poem goes on to explore whether "it" may be found in such mundane urban experience as "the act of buying . . . the girls crowding the stores, where light / colour, solid dreams are" (*CEP*, 29–30). This reference to the "solid dreams" of "girls crowding the stores" exemplifies a dynamic found throughout Levertov's early poetry, but especially in her poetry of urban experience: the dynamic of enclosure and release. In "Beyond the End" the "gay / desire" of shopping is tentatively portrayed as a vital activity, but such desire for release from the boredom of everyday life is more frequently presented as materialistic greed masquerading as the quest for "authentic" experience.[28]

Images of figures consumed by the very commercialist ideology that motivates them are countered by urban images of tentative release throughout Levertov's early New York poems. This dynamic is also frequently self-reflexive, as "February Evening in New York" exemplifies. This poem blends a moment of release, in this case from the workday, with a reflection on its own free-verse measure:

> As the buildings close, released autonomous
>   feet pattern the streets
>   in hurry and stroll . . .
>
> (*CEP*, 101)

This apparent qualification of her own gesture of autonomy—the "released autonomous / feet" portrayed as a mere reflex action—becomes a celebration of the city's collective "pattern" of movement toward a "range / of open time at winter's outskirts" (*CEP*, 101). The "released autonomous / feet," like the "girls crowding the stores" in "Beyond the End," find momentary respite in the illusion of their release. If "Beyond the End" does find an apparently authentic "grace" of "the grass, the humble rhythms, the / falling & rising of leaf and star" (*CEP*, 30), it nonetheless ironically undercuts its own quest for such aesthetic "grace," asking whether "it" can be found in the act of searching:

                                        every damn
craftsman has it while he's working
        but it's not
a question of work: some
shine with it, in repose. Maybe it is
response, the will to respond—("reason
can give nothing at all
like the response to desire") maybe
a gritting of the teeth, to go
just that much further, beyond the end
beyond whatever ends: to begin, to be, to defy.

                                        (*CEP*, 30)

"Response" and the "will to respond" ultimately cannot be differentiated, as the poem's final stanza responds to the thwarted quest for an
equivalent to the "natural" energy it has heretofore sought in social activity. The conclusion contradicts the claims it asserts: to end "beyond
the end" is to impose closure nonetheless. To defy "the end / beyond
whatever ends" is to temporarily accept one's limitations, to affirm one's
ability to persist in spite of frustration; but such defiance is also a renunciation of the totalizing proclamations, whether ethical or aesthetic,
as this poem seeks to "defy" even the quest to go "beyond the end" that
open-form poetics assume.

Poems about poetry like "Beyond the End" dramatize the poet's
struggle to compose, to discover meaningful patterns in everyday experience. Levertov frequently figures this struggle in images of enclosure
and release, whether they be the image of the bird temporarily trapped
within the poet's room in "The Flight" or more explicitly gendered
images of entrapment and escape in "The Goddess," "Matins," or "About
Marriage," which stresses the difference of "wedlock" from the idealized image of marriage as a meeting "in a green / airy space, not locked
in" (*P*, 141). "The Gypsy's Window," "The Whirlwind," and "The Palm
Tree" exemplify such poems that situate the dialectic of enclosure and
release within the confines of domestic space. In each of these poems
the poet is enclosed within her domestic/work space and struggles to
come to terms with an "outside" world that is either frustratingly inaccessible or overwhelmingly present, a distant "beyond" or a threatening
immanent "end." "The Gypsy's Window" enacts a release from the constricted domestic space of "the gypsy," a space concurrently containing
mysterious otherness and the poet's inescapable mirror image, first by

imaginatively inhabiting the "narrownecked vase" and "paper roses" with vibrant energy, and next by tossing the "chance of poetry" out of the window toward "dusty / Hudson St." This double act of acceding to confinement, of "making" something from the limitations of domestic experience, and of resisting such confinement, of making the gesture of "released autonomous feet," characterizes "The Whirlwind" and "The Palm Tree" as well. Both poems affirm the protection afforded by their confinement, but both also try to internalize the overwhelming power of the storm outside. Such patterns of enclosure and release typically resolve themselves not by simply affirming the immanent presence of the material world, as many of Levertov's critics claim, nor by simply affirming the poet's power to imaginatively order the world. Instead, these patterns frequently reach their unstable resolutions by reflecting on how subject-object relations are mediated, whether by the physical structures (the window, the wall) dividing/joining inside and outside, or the formal structures dividing/joining the poet and her intertexts. The attitude toward literary tradition demonstrated in these poems, when applied specifically to the masculinist, avant-garde stance of Williams, has the effect of deflating his claims for the primacy of formal innovation, while simultaneously foregrounding his generous commitment to an ideal of literary community. I would now like to return more specifically to Levertov's self-construction in the "Williams tradition," this time examining a poem that stresses the anxiety of separation more than the commitment to connection: her moving tribute to Pound, Williams, and H.D., "September 1961."

In "September 1961" Levertov laments the loss of "the old great ones," Pound, Williams, and H.D., who although "not dying," are "withdrawn into a painful privacy / learning to live without words" (P, 81). At this time, Pound was ill, Williams had had a cerebral hemorrhage, which made reading and writing difficult for him, and H.D. had suffered a stroke, which likewise made it difficult for her to communicate. This poem explores the process of learning to live with *their* words, and with their poetics, without their guiding presence, a process depicted in coinciding terms of anxiety and humility, confusion and clarity. The controlling trope of the poem, the road to the sea on which the poet meditates, follows the poetic line furthered by Pound, Williams, and H.D., but this continuity is disrupted by images that differentiate the poet's journey from the path she follows. The poem begins with an apparently straightforward acknowledgment of loss:

This is the year the old ones,
the old great ones
leave us alone on the road.

The road leads to the sea.

(P, 81)

The initial repetition of "old" accentuates the poet's empathetic reflection on old age, as she considers both their painful solitude and their now wordless worlds, and the feelings of loss and loneliness their decline provokes in her. The echoes of "old" with "road," and "old" with "alone," introduce the poem's concern with death, the "sea" that lies at the end of the road. Yet these first two sentences initiate another set of emotions that coincide with this sense of despair. The repetition of "old" to describe the "great" poets who have served as models for her work also evokes their passing authority as the "great ones." To "leave us alone" suggests the poet's sense of abandonment, although tempered by her assertion of solidarity with her fellow poets ("us" instead of "me"). But this loneliness coincides with a feeling of relief, in the colloquial sense of being "left alone," a sense of relief especially apt for Levertov's apprentice relationship with Williams, who never hesitated to offer her paternalistic advice.

Although Pound, Williams, and H.D. are no longer so vitally present as guides, teachers, or advisors, their successors nevertheless still have their written examples to follow: "We have words in our pockets, / obscure directions" (P, 81). These "obscure directions" carried in their "pockets" are in fact quite literally New Directions paperbacks, or pocketbooks. Such a playful yet subtle reference to her publisher celebrates Levertov's own inclusion in the company of the "old great ones," while conveying the significance of the circulation of these poets' names as literary "stars," far from the obscurity they had once shared. Yet this image of "words in our pockets" also initiates patterns of continuity and separation that the poem goes on to develop. To carry "words in our pockets," intimately close to one's body, protected, is to assert this poetry's importance for everyday life. The poem affirms not only an intellectual respect for the "obscure" words of these poets but a direct physical attachment that signifies their currency on the road as well as in the library.

The physical presence of the words handed down from the "old poets" to the new is reiterated several stanzas later, this time in terms of the responsibility for carrying on their work:

> They have told us
> the road leads to the sea,
> and given
>
> the language into our hands.
>
> (*P*, 82)

The tremendous responsibility to sustain the inherited "language," to follow the road to the sea with only "obscure directions," generates considerable anxiety for the poet's generation, as the succeeding passage demonstrates:

> We hear
> our footsteps each time a truck
>
> has dazzled past us and gone
> leaving us new silence.
>
> (*P*, 82)

As in the earlier description of the darkness left by the declining older generation of poets, "the horizon ringed with confused urban light-haze" (*P*, 81), solitude is here associated with the urban world, the world of commerce that confuses "the language," or more specifically, the place of poetry in the modern—and postmodernist—world. The intrusion of the commercial world, whether the distant vague "urban light-haze" or the present din of the "dazzling" truck, produces "new silence." This "new silence" is simultaneously a retreat from the avant-gardist aim to integrate poetry with the discordant rhythms of everyday life and a recognition of the newness of such silence. The "tradition of the new" can be both reaffirmed and transformed by the poet's refusal to either replicate or supersede the "footsteps" of the "old great ones":

> One can't reach
>
> the sea on this endless
> road to the sea unless
> one turns aside at the end, it seems,
>
> follows
> the owl that silently glides above it
> aslant, back and forth,

and away into deep woods.

(P, 82)

The figure of the owl gliding above the road "aslant" is an especially apt metaphor for Levertov's intertextual evocations of the "old great ones," but the "owl" connotes sorrow as well as wisdom. The only way to "reach / the sea" is to both accept the loss of certainty afforded by the road and to depart into "deep woods," to accept the mystery, darkness and confusion of the unconscious. Yet this move offers only a momentary respite to the poet's place in the dominant ethos of her age, as the return from "deep woods" explains:

> But for us the road
> unfurls itself, we count the
> words in our pockets, we wonder
> how it will be without them.

(P, 82–83)

The question of whether the poet can actually choose her road—whether "for us" implies "according to us" or "before us"—is left open. If the "road / unfurls itself" from its prior supports, the mentors to whom she pays homage, the "words in our pockets" are neither any less urgent nor any less "obscure" as directions for present action. The act of counting the words reiterates not only the self-consciousness of *following* open-form models but suggests an anxiety of losing the words, or of spending them. To "count the / words in our pockets" is to make sure their value still exists; however, the poet's act of self-consciously counting her words calls into question the valuation of poetry solely by its formal originality.

The road that Levertov has followed beyond "September 1961" has been, on the one side, more mystical and, on the other, more politically radical, an intensified aesthetic ethic that has to some degree sacrificed the "here and now" for the romantic spirit of quest. The "here and now" of the quest has, in other words, superseded the quest into the "here and now." Yet the "here and now" of her Williams imitations is not merely the "there and then" of early apprentice work. The conflicts between private and public roles for poetry, and between private and public visions within her poetry, that these poems dramatize are more fully resolved in such sequence poems as "A Common Ground," "Three

Meditations," and the "Olga Poems." As Levertov's radical political stance has informed her poetry since the 1960s, she has recuperated another Williams frequently overlooked by his imitators: Williams the political poet. The social vision of Williams's "energetic, compassionate, questioning spirit" is most evident in his early poetry, she argues, especially in such sequences as *Spring and All* and *The Descent of Winter*. The prevalent understanding of Williams as primarily an imagist or objectivist poet prevents "the experience of becoming aware precisely through the physical *presentness* of what is *de*noted, of the other presentness—invisible but palpable—of what is *con*noted," that is, "the ideas in the things."[29] Williams's poems on social issues epitomize what Levertov defines as the political poems of "active empathy," of "the projection of a nonparticipant into the experience of others very different from himself," as her Vietnam War protest poems themselves exemplify.[30] Most importantly, though, Levertov cites Williams to insist that any change in political consciousness must be formally successful in the poem; the political poem must "affect our senses and engage our aesthetic response just as much as one with whose contact . . . we can have no argument."[31] The ultimate goal of political poetry is to "attain to such osmosis of the personal and the public, of assertion and of song, that no one would be able to divide our poems into categories."[32] The politically committed writer would thus respond to the question "What is political poetry?" no differently than to the question "What is poetry?" Levertov's radical re-vision of her own poetics accentuates what her early imitations of Williams more tentatively assert, that "avant-garde," open-form writing can foreground patterns of connection rather than patterns of individuation, of community rather than solitude, and of empathy rather than detached observation.

5

"Going to sleep with quandariness": The "Post-anti-esthetic" Poetics of Frank O'Hara

And after all, only Whitman and Crane and Williams, of the American poets, are better than the movies.

—Frank O'Hara, "Personism: A Manifesto"

It's so
original, hydrogenic, anthropomorphic, fiscal, post-anti-esthetic,
     bland, unpicturesque and WilliamCarlosWilliamsian!
it's definitely not 19th century, it's not even Partisan Review, it's
     new, it must be vanguard!

—Frank O'Hara, "Poem Read at Joan Mitchell's"

In his "manifesto," originally written on request for *The New American Poetry*, O'Hara writes that "personism" was "founded by me after lunch with LeRoi Jones on August 27, 1959, a day in which I was in love with someone" (*CP*, 499).[1] By accentuating the moment in which this "movement" was "founded and which nobody knows about," this manifesto/ "diary" (*CP*, 510) mocks the pretentiousness of avant-gardist polemics. And by measuring the value of American poets by comparing them to the movies, he challenges the modernist distinction between high art and mass culture. Similarly, "Poem Read at Joan Mitchell's," O'Hara's celebration of Jane Freilicher's impending marriage to Joe Hazan, playfully inscribes his poetic stance within the "vanguard," as "it's" signifies not only the poem's occasion but the act of celebration itself. Like "Personism," "Poem Read at Joan Mitchell's" dramatizes a moment of emotional urgency: the fear of losing his close friendship with Jane Freilicher informs his subtle satire of the institution of marriage. Yet like so much of his poetry, this "occasional poem" self-consciously reflects on its own place in the "tradition of the new." The description of the marriage combines economic and aesthetic terms, situating this poetic act within the cultural politics of representing the "vanguard"; an "original" act, as the intensifier "so" implies, is original only insofar as it is mediated by definitions of the "new." The proper name describing this "original" marriage, "WilliamCarlosWilliamsian," epitomizes this recognition, for his name represents a site of contention in the 1950s "poetry wars," not only for his literary reputation but for the meaning of American modernism. This "WilliamCarlosWilliamsian" marriage mocks both O'Hara's affiliation with Williams's poetics and the objectification of his name as the commodity, "vanguard" writer. The parodic tone of this gesture furthermore suggests O'Hara's critique of the masculinist, Americanist stance associated with Williams's postwar protégés. Whether in mock-manifesto or mock-epithalamion, O'Hara's references to modern literary history—although seemingly offhand—challenge such influential claims as Helen Vendler's early overview that "the will *not* to impute significance has scarcely been stronger in lyric poetry."[2] In this chapter I will examine how O'Hara's "post-anti-esthetic" poetics of the quotidian enact a complex revision of the rhetoric of avant-gardism, especially that of Williams.

"Personism" and "Poem Read at Joan Mitchell's" exemplify the rhetoric of improvisation that characterizes O'Hara's writing. Yet his supposedly spontaneous responses to the historical moment recall the avant-gardist stances of such French poets as Baudelaire, Apollinaire, and Reverdy, as well as of the American poet Whitman. The twentieth-century American poetic stance that combines these two traditions, and that O'Hara frequently evokes, is Williams's, as comparing prominently located self-portraits of theirs will indicate. The first example is Williams's own version of the doctor-poet in the foreword to his *Autobiography*, while the second is O'Hara's back-cover statement for the City Lights "Pocket Poets" collection, *Lunch Poems:*

> Five minutes, ten minutes, can always be found. I had my typewriter in my office desk. All I had to do was to pull up the leaf to which it was fastened and I was ready to go. I worked at top speed. If a patient came in at the door while I was in the middle of a sentence, bang would go the machine—I was a physician. When the patient left, up would come the machine. My head developed a technique: something growing inside me demanded reaping. It had to be attended to . . . (*A*, xiii)

Often this poet, strolling through the noisy splintered glare of a Manhattan noon, has paused at a sample Olivetti to type up thirty or forty
lines of ruminations, or pondering more deeply has withdrawn to a darkened ware-or-fire-house to limn his computed misunderstandings of the
eternal questions of life, co-existence and depth, while never forgetting
to eat Lunch his favorite meal . . .[3]

Williams's self-portrait is marked by a compulsion to compose that transcends the time restraints imposed by his fitful physician's schedule:
"Five minutes, ten minutes, can always be found." O'Hara's self-portrait likewise represents the act of writing as inextricably bound to the
schedule of the daily workplace; however, Williams's writing is more
organically related to his job. The typewriter is attached to the doctor's
desk as his patients become the subjects of his poems. If the two roles
of doctor and poet are figured as mechanically separate activities—"bang
would go the machine . . . up would come the machine"—the metaphor
for composing itself evokes Williams's obstetric practice: "[S]omething
growing inside me demanded reaping." O'Hara's self-portrait, on the
other hand, does not even mention his job at the Museum of Modern
Art, although the "noisy splintered glare of a Manhattan noon" does
suggest a modernist aestheticizing of this site for composing, while the
"sample Olivetti" underlines the commodification of the poet's "machine." The lunch break itself, the hour contained yet liminally outside
the restrictions of the employer's time clock, replaces the five minutes
between patients.

   Williams's emphasis on speed, spontaneity, improvisation, and vir-
tuosity is supported by a conviction that poetry and medicine inform
the same humanistic project, that writing a poem and diagnosing a patient are intimately related activities. O'Hara's melodramatic tone mocks
Williams's certainty of purpose, but it also registers mild despair at the
loss of faith in universalizing ethical, scientific, and aesthetic principles.
The sense of casual desperation in the poet "withdrawn to a darkened
ware-or-fire-house to limn his computed misunderstandings" underscores the ironic tone that makes the "eternal questions of life, co-existence and depth" both compelling and laughable. O'Hara's tone of crisis
is informed by an acute sensitivity to cold-war historical conditions,
especially to the oppressive mechanisms that an ideology that represses
difference can deploy.[4] And his tone evokes the more general threat
of nuclear annihilation, a threat which paradoxically levels distinctions

between kinds of experiences while heightening awareness of the ephem-erality of the quotidian—there is no guarantee that "five minutes, ten minutes, can always be found." The progressivist faith in technology and technique that animates Williams's avant-gardist dictum to "make it new" can no longer be asserted unproblematically.

O'Hara's readers often note the exemplary importance of Williams's formal devices, as well as his more general struggle against convention, pretentiousness, and conformity in his commitment to the vernacular and celebration of the quotidian.[5] However, none of O'Hara's readers fully accounts for his intertextual evocations of the avant-gardist stance whose critical edge he seeks to retain, yet whose critical mode appears inadequate for addressing postwar American historical conditions. Whereas the Black Mountain poets and Beats tend to reinscribe Williams's Americanist and masculinist assumptions, O'Hara subjects these assumptions to critical scrutiny. For O'Hara, Williams's value lies in his sustained attempt to mediate the critical stance of the European avant-garde with the specific historical conditions of modernization in twentieth-century American culture. Williams's early lyrics and the prose poetry of *Kora in Hell* are his most compelling models.[6] This poetry most radically dramatizes modern subjectivity as the unstable locus of intersecting discourses, as the combination of a rhetoric of discovery, a structure of free-verse and open forms, and a thematic concern with the local and the quotidian highlights the intersection of the political with the personal in everyday life. The Williams that O'Hara parodies in his self-portrait for *Lunch Poems* is not the experimental poet of the 1920s New York avant-garde, however. O'Hara engages in this general struggle for the significance of Williams's poetics in his project of recuperating an avant-gardist Williams. But in doing so, he measures his own dis-tance from the New York avant-garde of the 1910s and 20s, as well as from the Williams being reread in American universities as a major American modernist poet. O'Hara's project is thus defined by a con-tinuous process of examining the relevance of modern literary history to his postwar historical moment, a process that tends to be ignored in summaries of his relationship to Williams.

As O'Hara's parodic evocation of Williams's stance suggests, read-ing his poetics in a continuous tradition of indeterminacy or imma-nence raises important questions about the continuity of an avant-garde "tradition."[7] While formulations of postmodernism tend to dispute how postmodernist texts reflect or subvert the social effects of postwar capitalism, they generally agree that postmodernist and modernist aesthetics can be differentiated by their positions toward the past. For example, Fredric Jameson has argued that postmodernism's "commitment to surface and the *superficial*" signifies a retreat from the "protopolitical vocation and the terrorist stance of the older modernism."[8] In distinguishing pastiche from parody, he argues that postmodernist art thematizes the failure of the modernist project. Given the eclipse of conditions for modernist stylistic innovation—i.e., of individualism and of any linguistic norm with which to contrast styles—postmodernist imitation lacks any satirical impulse. Instead of parody, pastiche is thus the only possible mode for responding to the past: "All that is left is to imitate dead styles, to speak through the masks and through the voices of the styles in the imaginary museum. But this means that contemporary or postmodernist art is going to be about art itself in a new kind of way; even more, it means that one of its essential messages will involve the necessary failure of art and the aesthetic, the failure of the new, the imprisonment in the past."[9] Jameson's formulation accurately describes the play of allusion and quotation on the textual surface of a writer like O'Hara. However, O'Hara's writing represents less of an "imprisonment in the past" than the recognition that history is accessible only through its representations. If O'Hara's multivalent texts suggest that style is not freely expressed but is written through cultural codes, they also reveal that history is not a given that is immediately accessible by allusion, but must be always constructed. Furthermore, Jameson's totalizing formulation of postmodernism as a cultural dominant, following Ernest Mandel's socioeconomic periodization, obscures how postmodernist practices often retain the avant-gardist oppositional impulse while rejecting the formalist notion of textual autonomy, as Andreas Huyssen and Linda Hutcheon have argued.[10]

Informed by his prominent position within the New York art-publishing and museum world, O'Hara's poetry invokes a dialogical relation between past traditions and the present that is more analogous to Charles Jencks's examples of postmodernist architecture and Hutcheon's examples of "historiographic metafiction" than to politically marked postmodernist practices. Jencks argues that postmodernist architecture subverts modernist aestheticism through a process of "double coding," an interplay of modernist technique with allusion to popular traditions to communicate both with "experts" and a more general public audience.[11] The "expert" readers of O'Hara—literary critics and historians—concentrate exclusively on the narrative surface of his poetry precisely because his process of double coding challenges this dichotomy of experts and public. Many of his most obscurely autobiographical texts also participate in the general project of rewriting modern literary history. While his poetry appeals to a general audience through its recognizable narrative structures, it challenges "experts" to become conversant with the details of his life, especially within the New York art world and the gay community, as well as with modern literary history. In stressing the moment and site of enunciation, and frequently the specific receiver as well as the sender of the poetic text, O'Hara subverts the expertise of literary critics while enhancing the value of "local" knowledge.

An early O'Hara poem that cogently, although obliquely, evokes the postwar crisis of historical memory that Jameson associates with the postmodern is "Memorial Day 1950." This "pastiche" of modernist styles critically interrogates the concept of the "vanguard," anticipating O'Hara's more specific, more explicit practice and explanations of intertextuality in his later lyric poetry and criticism. Marjorie Perloff praises this poem, written during O'Hara's final year at Harvard, as a breakthrough that adumbrates his later distinctive poetic achievement, the fusion of the surrealist "dialectic of polarized images" with the colloquial diction of Williams.[12] Yet this poem not only replicates the avant-gardist techniques of the artists it names, it enacts an interrogation of the subtexts relating modernism and modernity. From the poem's title—specifying a moment of reflection at the midpoint of the twentieth century—until its enigmatic yet apocalyptic conclusion, "Memorial Day 1950" fuses and confuses personal memory with codified historical memory, personal desire with textual knowledge, imagination with recollection. The title memorializes not only the moment of reflection but the moments reflected on, from the reflection on the war dead designated by the official holiday to the poet's reflection on his biological and literary "parents." In what seem like random associations between fractured literary fragments and recollections of childhood trauma, the poem explores the structures of feeling linking aesthetic avant-gardism with military avant-gardism. While mocking the self-aggrandizing posture of both the aesthetic manifesto and the bildungsroman, the poem conveys a version of modern literary history that acknowledges the rhetorical appeal of avant-gardist utopianism while questioning the corresponding impulse to destroy past accomplishments. In parodying modernist texts, it mocks its own destructive impulse. In leaving the poet's attitude toward his modernist predecessors ambivalent, "Memorial Day 1950" engages its readers in questioning how aesthetic forms represent modes for interpreting history.

The semantic instability of "Memorial Day 1950" begins with its cryptic opening sentence:

> Picasso made me tough and quick, and the world;
> just as in a minute plane trees are knocked down
> outside my window by a crew of creators.

(CP, 17)

Here we can see the formal devices O'Hara adapts from Williams: the syntactic ambiguity of ordinary words and phrases, combined later in the poem with continuous enjambment, creates a tension of rapidly shifting surfaces. The comma that separates "and the world" from the initial clause is especially puzzling, as it raises questions concerning both the production and the reception of complex artistic texts. What is the status of "made" in this clause? Do we locate the semantic stress on the act of making, the "made" text, or the audience "made . . . tough and quick" by the text? Did Picasso make "me . . . and the world," thus implying the poet's total identification with Picasso's made world? Or is he maintaining some distance from Picasso while affirming the *effects* of his painting? Such interpretive questions are specific to complex artistic texts, but they also foreground the interpreter's historical difference. To consider Picasso in 1950 calls into question the relation of cubist aesthetics to modern warfare posited by such commentaries as Gertrude Stein's: "I very well remember at the beginning of the war being with Picasso on the boulevard Raspail when the first camouflage truck passed. It was at night, we had heard of camouflage but we had not yet seen it and Picasso amazed looked at it and then cried out, yes it is we who made it, that is cubism."[13] Furthermore, it is impossible to read "Picasso," perhaps *the* signifier for the international avant-garde, without acknowledging the diverse appropriations of his aesthetics and his name. As the poem's parody of Stein's syntax and diction suggests, the effect of Picasso's multiple technical revolutions on the poet's own development cannot be severed from the objectification of Picasso as a cultural icon. The opening line of "Memorial Day 1950" dramatizes the semantic instability of avant-gardist texts through its fractured syntax;

the conclusion of this opening sentence, although an apparently straight-forward statement, becomes more questionable in its equation of destruction and creation. The textualized trees, "in a minute plane" of the cubist surface, fuse with the "plane trees . . . outside my window." The mundane act of knocking down trees to "create" a new landscape, an act epitomizing bourgeois progressivism, evolves into the image of Picasso the ax-wielder. In the understated tone of this first verse paragraph, the poem establishes a problematic affiliation of avant-gardist manifesto rhetoric with the rhetoric of warfare: to "fight" for the "rubbish" left by the "creators" asserts the value of the quotidian and the demotic for artistic texts, but only because the context of modern warfare animates our awareness of such value.

It could be argued that "Memorial Day 1950" is hardly surrealist at all, that the images of artistic production, warfare, and bourgeois family life follow an internal logic of violent rebellion that deconstructs the poles of destruction and creation. However, the poem does not follow consistently logical rhetorical patterns. Its generative principle appears to arise from the exhaustion felt by the artist in the wake of the historical avant-garde, as the references to Gertrude Stein and Max Ernst early in the poem imply. Such allusions to what has already been said convey a postmodernist anxiety that formal innovation is no longer possible and, furthermore, that the world wars have achieved the act of revolutionary destruction that avant-gardist rhetoric called for. The postwar artist must then accept a role analogous to that of Alice B. Toklas, the "autobiographical" subject constructed by Stein, as the poet is "made" by Picasso. The remainder of the poem enacts this process of literary ventriloquism, as the names and quotes of Klee, Auden, Rimbaud, Pasternak, and Apollinaire, among others, comically reverberate through the fragments of battles the young poet has with his parents. In fusing avant-gardist models of rebellion with the recollections of his own adolescent rebellion, O'Hara imparts an absurd sense of the quotidian to these artists whose earlier transformations of everyday life had earned them a monumental status by 1950. And in situating these fragmentary fusings of manifestos and family disputes in the bloodshed of modern warfare, O'Hara conveys an urgency to his poem's articulation of its own historical moment.

"Memorial Day 1950" enacts a process of appropriation and distancing from O'Hara's modernist predecessors, as one of its buried narratives, the transformation of Picasso's "The Man with the Blue

Guitar," epitomizes. At first the original "maker," Picasso is invoked through the name of his painting, *Guernica*. The poet then figures himself as the artist in "tight blue pants," as he confronts his disapproving parents. His parents are then generalized as the "older people" who come into his room and break both his guitar and his can of blue paint. The figure made by Picasso becomes the maker, the man with the blue paint, as well as the made, the man with the guitar. By the poem's conclusion, however, the "guitar strings" serve the more mundane but crucial purpose of holding up the artist's "pictures." Through this process of distancing himself from the maker of "The Man with the Blue Guitar," O'Hara does not reject the technical accomplishments of a Picasso, not to mention a Wallace Stevens; rather, he rejects the definition of art that limits the object to its exchange value as a commodity. In figuring his own poetic stance as an improvisational act of holding up pictures with guitar strings, O'Hara portrays the postmodernist representation of the past as a mode of bricolage. "Memorial Day 1950" is indeed a pastiche of avant-gardist rhetoric, yet its parodic play on modes of rebellion underscores the complex historicity of any aesthetic, including (and especially) that of its own.

If "Memorial Day 1950" exemplifies the technical achievement of O'Hara's later depictions of the present moment, its construction of recent history informs his occasional writings on his contemporaries in both the literary and visual arts. In differentiating between the European notion of avant-gardism and its American counterpart, he claims that European art treats the aesthetic and the political as equally important distinct categories, whereas American art combines the aesthetic with the political, which creates its "metaphysical quality."[14] Yet this does not mean that art in America serves no social function. Citing Gregory Corso's poem, "Bomb," he writes: "And it is the character of the avant-garde to absorb and transform disparate qualities not normally associated with art, for the artist to take within him the violence and evil of his times and come out with something. . . . In this way society can bear and understand and finally appreciate the qualities of alien and even dangerous things."[15] This description of the avant-garde's relation to "society" corresponds with O'Hara's understanding of how the avant-gardist stance is internalized. In a 1965 interview with Edward Lucie-Smith, he generalizes that the avant-garde is not defined by a political or socioeconomic condition of detachment or isolation. When artists such as Andy Warhol become celebrities, he says, such a stance is absurd: "[T]here's no reason to attack a culture that will allow it to happen, and even foster the impulse—and create it. Which is a *change*, you see, from the general idea . . . that all avant-garde art has to be attacking the bourgeoisie."[16] Since postwar American capitalism contains opposition to the extent that the marketplace even encourages it, the avant-gardist impulse for innovation no longer plays a viable critical role. What becomes most important, then, is how art positions itself within traditions of innovation and, in doing so, transforms our perception of past forms. O'Hara's monograph on Jackson Pollock is especially instructive for explaining this conception of intertextuality.

There is nothing unusual about situating the urgency of Pollock's "action painting" in the context of cold-war tensions, but the terms of O'Hara's analysis are rarely considered in relation to his own poetic practice: "[I]t is not surprising that faced with universal destruction, as we are told, our art should at last speak with unimpeded force and unveiled honesty to a future which well may be non-existent, in a last effort of recognition which is the justification of being."[17] Pollock's painting thus responds to the inescapable demands of the historical moment with a heightened sensitivity to the passing of time. His paintings are "painfully beautiful celebrations of what will disappear, or has disappeared already, from his world, or what may be destroyed at any moment."[18] If Pollock's method of painting represents a process fundamentally different from that of previous generations of modern painters, it is because his world compels a reconception of history. The postwar threat of imminent annihilation represents an unprecedented scale of apocalypse, for the destruction of the entire world indeed becomes as fundamentally possible as the destruction of the individual body. Action Painting's mode for internalizing this sense of crisis is its revolutionary use of scale. The scale of the painting becomes the scale of the painter's body, and the setting for the scale becomes the canvas surface itself. And foregrounding the act of painting preserves the act of resistance to totalizing systems in its historical specificity. For O'Hara's poetics breath becomes the physiological analogy to the painter's body as a compositional force.[19] Foregrounding the act of enunciation similarly enacts resistance to totalizing systems, including those of closed poetic forms.

What ultimately distinguishes O'Hara's interpretation of Pollock from the conventional image of the heroically destructive modern artist is his emphasis on how Pollock's painting preserves what is valuable in previous traditions of painting. Differentiating Pollock's "spirited revaluation" of modern painting from Arshile Gorky's more destructive mode of "assimilation," he writes that Pollock

> did not appropriate . . . what was beautiful, frenzied, ugly or candid in others, but enriched it and flung it back to their work, as if it were a re-interpretation for the benefit of all, a clarification and apotheosis which does not destroy the things seen, whether of nature or art, but preserves it in a pure regard. Very few things, it seems, were assimilated or absorbed by Pollock. They were left intact, and given back. Paint is paint, shells and wire are shells and wire, glass is glass, canvas is canvas. You do not find, in his work, a typewriter becoming a stomach, a sponge becoming a brain.[20]

Although his formulation is analogous to T. S. Eliot's familiar concept of intertextuality in "Tradition and the Individual Talent," O'Hara not only rejects the priority of a canonical tradition of high art but emphasizes the way artistic texts transform our perception of the world, or "nature," as well as our perception of previous texts. Pollock's painting retains the materials, techniques, and imagery of modern art, but they are transformed by his interpretation: the past takes on "reality for us outside his work, as a cultural by-product of his own achievement."[21] With this emphasis on the historicity of formal innovation, the act of preservation he attributes to Pollock involves a nondestructive, nonadversarial attitude to the past that differs from the historical avant-garde as well as from Eliot's high modernism. Furthermore, Pollock's oeuvre exposes the limitations of reductive definitions of "tradition" or "the individual talent." In noting that artists who succeed in sustaining a "multiplicity of truths" in a multiplicity of styles are "met with the accusation of 'no coherent, unifying style,' rather than a celebration,"[22] O'Hara could be answering his own critics. His formulation of Pollock's intertextual "revaluation" of past traditions is especially appropriate for reinterpreting his relation to his modernist predecessors. I will now concentrate on one key example of O'Hara's "revaluation" of avant-gardism—the example of his revision of Williams's objectivist poetics—to show how his appropriations of Williams's form, prosody, syntax, and diction play a role similar to Pollock's in accentuating the historical transmission of aesthetic forms.

O'Hara's poetry of the late 1940s and early 1950s is marked by numerous "appropriations" of Williams's formal strategies and thematic concerns, but even these instances contain parodic elements that foresee his "revaluation" of Williams's poetics in his "I do this I do that" poems. O'Hara's poetry of these years as an undergraduate and graduate student includes explicit parody of the period's dominant modes, from direct mockery of Eliot in "Poem" ("Let's take a walk you") to a more generalized parody of academic verse in "Poem" ("The ivy is trembling in the hammock"). His parodies of Williams, however, are more subtle and less overtly sarcastic. In addition to appropriating Williams's poetic form, prosody, syntax, and diction, O'Hara also responds to the philosophical assumptions of Williams's poetics. "A Sort of a Song," the introductory poem in Williams's influential collection *The Wedge*, is a sort of a summary of his poetics, and we can examine O'Hara's response to Williams's stance in a poem entitled "Today." Its title accentuating its historicity, O'Hara's poem "Today" answers the conclusion of "A Sort of a Song," Williams's demand for "No ideas / but in things," with a motley assortment of objects, such as "kangaroos, sequins," and "chocolate sodas," "stuff" that "still makes a poem a surprise" (*CP*, 15). This collection of objects seems to be related only randomly; what initially makes this poem a surprise is the fact that this "stuff" is hardly the "things" to which Williams refers, and certainly not things that make a poem a "small machine made of words." Yet what ultimately makes this short poem a surprise is its concluding shift in tone, as O'Hara's objects are located on "beachheads" and "biers" (*CP*, 15). The association of this "stuff" with war and death compels us to reconsider their significance, as the poem's title, "Today," refers to the immediate postwar years. Rather than defamiliarizing the everyday, "Today" foregrounds the ephemerality of everyday "stuff," including everyday language; the objects seem to be linked as much by the sonorous sequence of names as by appeal to any readily apparent semantic codes. The poem affirms the meaning of things, but refuses to impose a recognizable order on them. The use of *stuff* to summarize these objects seems to flaunt the lack of specificity involved in using colloquial language. It raises the question of whether these objects are the "stuff" of which this poem is made or the "stuff" from which a poem may yet be made, engaging readers to question their role in producing the poem's meaning. The semantic range of *stuff* itself recalls the war, but its connotations of drugs, other forms of contraband, and even of literary or journalistic copy call into question the rhetorical function of the poetic image. As if in direct response to "A Sort of a Song"—"through metaphor to reconcile / the people and the stones" (*CP 2*, 55)—"Today" exerts no demonstrative control over readers' interpretations of the sequence of objects. In relinquishing the will to power—Williams's metaphor of "saxifrage," which "splits / the rocks" (ibid.)—"Today" affirms not things in themselves, but the dialogue inherent in interpreting the codes that inform this surprising network of names and our conceptions of poetry's relation to the world of "today."

From the playful subversion of interpretive authority in "Today" to the similarly time-conscious but more satirical rewriting of "A Sort of a Song" in "Poetry," to the mockery of dogma in "To A Poet"—"and when the doctor comes to / me he says 'No things but in ideas'" (*CP*, 185)—O'Hara's early parodies of "A Sort of a Song" exemplify the prominence of his "appropriation" of Williams's technique. They also exemplify the significance of O'Hara's wartime experience for his ironic interpretation of the 1950s "poetry wars."[23] The transformation of Williams's poetics suggested in these poems subtly informs the poetry more frequently associated with O'Hara as well: the "I do this I do that" poems highlighted in the self-portrait for *Lunch Poems*. In these poems O'Hara's postmodernist "revaluation" of Williams's poetics calls into question the philosophical and ideological assumptions of the avant-gardist rhetoric informing his project. In reading O'Hara's poetic depictions of his contemporary New York art world as a revision of avant-gardism, especially Williams's paradoxical "localist" avant-gardism, it becomes evident that the familiar image of the spontaneous, unreflective poet mystifies O'Hara's engagement with the ideological and historical conditions that makes such a poetic stance a critique of New Critical reading practices.

O'Hara's statements about his composition habits have contributed to this image of the spontaneous, unreflective poet. He has said that he does not believe in revising poems, that he is most satisfied when "something falls into place as if it were a conversation or something."[24] The poem as "conversation" is fundamental to O'Hara's poetics, as "Poetry" implies, yet even this interview response reveals a cognizance of the constructedness of such a stance, "*as if it were* a conversation." O'Hara's skeptical, sarcastic, even flippant attitude toward his own poetry conceals a more self-conscious awareness of the implications of his technique. The "statement" for *The New American Poetry* that he substituted for "Personism" typifies his ironic circumspection, as he considers the relation of poetry to "life": "It may be that poetry makes life's nebulous events tangible to me and restores their detail; or conversely, that poetry brings forth the intangible quality of incidents which are all too concrete and circumstantial. Or each on specific occasions, or both all the time" (*CP*, 500). O'Hara hardly answers the question of how poetry represents "events" or "incidents," the "as if it were" aspect of his poems. He also refuses to say whether poetry "imputes significance" merely by the act of attention or naming. O'Hara's refusal to specify how a poem is significant or makes events significant transfers the act of attention to the reader. There is minimal subordination of seemingly insignificant elements to greater patterns of meaning in O'Hara's "I do this I do that" poems. Because these poems are narrative, the sequencing of events often overshadows any pattern of symbolic meaning. Although such poems resemble what Roland Barthes would call the classical "readerly" text in their apparently straightforward narrative structure, they continually submit the narrated events to questions concerning their ideological significance, concurring with Barthes's notion of structure in the "writerly" text: "[S]tructure is not a design, a schema, a diagram: everything signifies something."[25] The two polar hypotheses describing O'Hara's poetry—the "will *not* to impute significance"[26] and "everything signifies something"—inform the process of "double coding" that compels readers to continually decide on what is significant while concurrently reflecting on the grounds for such decisions. Such tension makes readers simultaneously attentive to significance in the seemingly insignificant and wary about attributing significance at all, as closer examination of several representative "I do this I do that poems" will show.

The poem that best illustrates this tension of attention is "The Day Lady Died," probably the poem most frequently cited for demonstrating O'Hara's antipoetic stance. Because this poem is an elegy, it is somewhat atypical of the more casual "I do this I do that" poems. The occasion of the poem, the death of Billie Holliday, heightens the significance of the poem's details. Nevertheless, the relation of the details to the poem's generic form remains problematic. The majority of critics agree that the details observed by the poem's speaker are random, that there is little significance to the times, people, places, and events mentioned. These details are the poem's "anti-poetic weight"[27] or mere coincidences that contrast sharply with the seriousness of the occasion. Robert von Hallberg's assessment that the poem's impact depends on its "inadvertent banal approach to an earnest genre" typifies this critical reaction.[28]

On the other hand, critics such as Charles Altieri have argued that the details of the poem do contribute to the feeling of the elegy.[29] Such critics still maintain the contrast between the discontinuity of the reported experiences and the poem's elegiac conclusion. Despite this disagreement about the poem's details to its impact as an elegy, no one is willing to read too much significance into the details; the sense that the poet seems to just coincidentally and randomly notice these details forecloses such conjecture.

"The Day Lady Died" epitomizes the tension between first and second readings of O'Hara's "I do this I do that" poems. Except for the cryptic title, a title whose significance would be noticed only by those familiar with Billie Holliday, there is no indication that the poem is an elegy until the closing stanza. Like so many of O'Hara's poems, "The Day Lady Died" narrates events in the present tense; the events occur concurrently with the utterance itself. This process of simultaneous composition is less stream-of-consciousness than consciousness-of-stream, the stream of urban streets reported in rapid succession. The rapidity of reporting, emphasized through paratactic syntax, constant enjambment, and minimal punctuation, precludes attention to detail. It is only with the poem's apocalyptic closure—"everyone and I stopped breathing" (CP, 325)—closure that unites the remembered event with the present, the performance of Holliday's song with the performance of the poem, that the narrated events become significant. Yet even when the poem has "stopped breathing," the details do not fit into a readily apparent design other than that of the speaker's lunchtime walk itself. The genre of the poem demands the reconstruction of design from its disparate details, but the details resist such reconstruction. To insist on a coherent design that unites the apparently random details is to risk reading too much symbolism into a poem whose tone is so casual; to avoid such a risk means accepting the cliché of the spontaneous, unreflective poet.

There are a number of references to time in "The Day Lady Died," typical for the lunch poems O'Hara wrote with one eye on his wristwatch but particularly significant for a poem about death. These references to time are hardly uniform, however; there is quite a difference between saying "It is 12:20 in New York a Friday" and saying "three days after Bastille Day" (CP, 325). The first reference situates the poem in a specific yet repeatable time frame, while the second calls attention to the poet's selection of a dramatic descriptive term. "Bastille Day" gives the poem a sense of historical depth that contrasts with the matter-of-fact reporting of departure and arrival times of the Long Island trains the poet plans to take that evening. The reference to Bastille Day hardly seems gratuitous, for many of the poem's succeeding historical and geographical references are to oppression, imprisonment, and revolution, issues intimately related to Billie Holliday's life. When the poet buys "an ugly NEW WORLD WRITING to see what the poets / in Ghana are doing these days" (CP, 325), he refers to a country (formerly the Gold Coast) that had gained independence in 1957, only two years before the "day Lady died." The reference to Ghana, rather than to another African country, is especially relevant for Holliday's African American genealogy, for the Gold Coast had been an important center for the slave trade. Similarly, the books the poet considers buying for "Patsy" are relevant for the final years of Holliday's life, years in which she was trailed by the FBI. The books mentioned, "Brendan Behan's new play or Le Balcon or Les Nègres / of Genet" (CP, 325), concern oppression and rebellion, and the authors were not only noted rebels but had spent time in prison themselves: Behan was twice imprisoned while a member of the IRA, Jean Genet spent much of his life in jails, and Paul Verlaine, whose book the speaker finally decides to buy, spent two years in a Belgian prison after shooting his lover, Arthur Rimbaud. As casual and coincidental as such references to authors and literary texts appear, the pattern of oppression and rebellion they convey casts a powerful shadow over a life the poem elegizes but never explicitly describes.

The other names the poet mentions—names of friends, familiar places, and consumer products—become more resonant with their historicity when juxtaposed to other historical periods, people, and places. The juxtaposition of names and places the poet knows closely ("Patsy," "Mike," "the GOLDEN GRIFFIN," the PARK LANE / Liquor Store," the "Ziegfeld Theatre," "the 5 SPOT") with historical figures and foreign places personalizes the poem's historical references. The mention of those the poet hardly knows at all ("the people who will feed me," "Miss Stillwagon") along with the mention of international trade names ("Strega," "Gauloises," "Picayunes") conflates the impersonal and the international with the personal and the local. As the literary and artistic center of 1950s American culture, New York offers unlimited choice, but only in exchange for the reified subjectivity of consumer capitalism. Finally, except for the reference to Bastille Day, all of the poem's references to "foreign" and "past" history (the poem as well as consumer capitalism problematize the meaning of foreign and past) are references to texts. History is always represented, in this case bracketed between the covers of the journals and books the poet browses through at newsstands and in bookstores. Even the first mention of the figure the poem celebrates appears in a "NEW YORK POST with her face on it" (CP, 325). This emphasis on the textuality of history foregrounds the relation of this literary text, "The Day Lady Died," to its immediate historical referent, the day "Lady" died. "The Day Lady Died" is concurrently a repeatable, ahistorical script and an unrepeatable historical transcript of events; the poem loses much of its resonance without historical knowledge of the day it records. In accentuating historical difference, the transience of the local people, places, and events named, the poem also suggests patterns of historical repetition: revolution in France and revolution in Ghana, persecution of artists in France and persecution of artists in America. By placing the death of Billie Holliday in the context of Bastille Day and official oppression of artists, O'Hara subtly comments on the state of the "avant-garde" artist in 1950s America.

All of the actions represented in "The Day Lady Died" are acts of selection, especially the consumer's selection of what to do and what to buy for specific social occasions. Most of these are automatic or socially constrained acts of selection, but beginning with the decision of the bank teller, "Miss Stillwagon," to not "even look up my balance for once in her life" (CP, 325), the process of selection raises fundamental interpretive questions. The poet does not speculate on "Miss Stillwagon's" reasons for her change of behavior, but by stressing the singularity of this occasion, he suggests his own act of reflection and encourages readers to consider the significance of the bank scene to the rest of the poem, and even the semantic possibilities of "Miss Stillwagon" and "my balance." The next act of selection initially seems to be as unproblematic as the other purchases: "and in the GOLDEN GRIFFIN I get a little Verlaine / for Patsy" (CP, 325). However, this seemingly unreflective act is modified by the catalog of book titles the poet has already considered, a catalog that concludes with the striking oxymoron: "I stick with Verlaine / after practically going to sleep with quandariness" (CP, 325). "Quandariness" implies a state of agitated or distressed awareness, a state not normally associated with sleep. "Going to sleep with quandariness" suggests a weariness with selection, in this case the consumer's weariness with selecting a literary text to give to his friend, but a weariness as well with selecting the appropriate literary references to elegize Holliday. On the other hand, "going to sleep" also suggests an erotic of "quandariness," as this weariness is belied by the inventiveness of such a line as "going to sleep with quandariness." The poem asserts that imaginative inventiveness can subvert imprisonment in tradition; likewise art can momentarily release one from the imprisonment of self-consciousness inherent in such anxiety of selection.

The final act of selection in "The Day Lady Died" appears not to be a conscious choice at all; the photograph of "Lady Day" invokes a memory of the artist's power to literally take one's breath away, and in doing so, to make the scenario of the poem's closure more vivid, more lasting. When the poem ends on this note, it not only closes the process of selection but heightens the significance of the poem's details as well. As the image of "Lady Day" conjures the precise memory of "leaning on the john door in the 5 SPOT" (*CP*, 325), the conclusion of "The Day Lady Died" sharpens the images portrayed earlier. Such lines as "and I don't know the people who will feed me" or "Miss Stillwagon . . . doesn't even look up my balance" (*CP*, 325) become laden with possibly ominous significance when viewed through the lens of Billie Holliday's death, a lens colored by the questions of oppression, revolt, and imprisonment that inform the references to other artists in the poem. It is possible to go to "sleep with quandariness" with the details of "The Day Lady Died" only by refusing to select how they are significant. Such a reading risks falling into a state of historical amnesia that the poem insistently militates against.

Because the elegiac closure of "The Day Lady Died" so thoroughly transforms all that happens before it, it is not the ideal example for examining the tension between "the wish not to impute significance" and "everything signifies something" in O'Hara's "I do this I do that" poems. In other "I do this I do that" poems the concern with time and death is less specifically motivated. "Personal Poem," for example, typifies the circular structure of many of these poems. It begins at lunchtime, depicts in the present tense events that occur or are discussed during lunch, and closes at the end of the lunch hour, when the poet goes to "buy a strap for my wristwatch" (*CP*, 336). Consequently, as in "The Day Lady Died," time becomes a recurring concern. The poem begins as if it were in the middle of an autobiography: "Now when I walk around at lunch time / I have only two charms in my pocket" (*CP*,

335). "Now" implies a past that differs from the present, while "only two charms" implies a sense of depletion, of loss. This initial sense of a fall is reinforced when the poet says, "but now I'm happy for a time and interested," and later, "the last five years my batting average / is .016 that's that" (CP, 335). This dark sense of loss, so characteristic of O'Hara's later poems, is not merely personal; "LeRoi" provides a political correlative for the poet's personal loss:

> and LeRoi comes in
> and tells me Miles Davis was clubbed 12
> times last night outside BIRDLAND by a cop
> a lady asks us for a nickel for a terrible
> disease but we don't give her one we
> don't like terrible diseases.
>
> (CP, 335)

The casual, matter-of-fact, even humorous description of disease and violence, once again official violence against a black jazz musician, conceals a darker sense of despair inherent in "but I'm happy for a time and interested" (CP, 335). Finally, with the companionship of LeRoi Jones, the transition from "I" to "we," the sense of despair is temporarily alleviated. Their discussion of literature, in which they ally themselves with Herman Melville and Don Allen rather than with figures associated with high-modernist aesthetics, Henry James and Lionel Trilling, leaves the speaker with the confidence that "one person of the 8,000,000 is / thinking of me" (CP, 336). Even this qualified optimism that ends the poem cannot hide the darker mood that situates the poet's own sense of isolation both diachronically in American literary history, with the affiliation with Melville, and synchronically on the streets of Manhattan. Thus even a passing descriptive phrase like "the construction to / the left that closed the sidewalk" (CP, 335) locates the progressivist assumptions of such "construction" in a context of police brutality and poverty. The image affirmed in the final verse paragraph—the poets as construction workers who "walk on girders in our silver hats" (CP, 336)—insists on "construction," on creation, on dialogue, but it also evokes an ideological subtext for the perilousness of walking on girders, of destruction, of silence.

Another poem that conveys its preoccupation with time and death through the transience of the lunch break is "A Step Away From Them." Whereas "Personal Poem" is more concerned with the interplay of the political with the personal in the contemporary "avant-garde," "A Step Away From Them" affiliates 1950s "vanguard" art with the historical avant-garde. The preoccupation with time opens the poem, with the announcement, "It's my lunch hour." It reappears soon after, when the poet looks at "bargains in wristwatches," is ironically suggested in the reference to Times Square, and explicitly signals the transition from present impressions to reflection on darkness and death, which takes place exactly at "12:40" (CP, 257). The images and actions described in the opening two verse paragraphs—shirtless laborers eating sandwiches, skirts "flipping / above heels," cats "playing in sawdust," a "Negro" smiling at a "chorus girl" (ibid.)—counteract the concern with time with their sensual vitality; they occur in rapid succession, in short enjambed sentences. The details of the urban scene draw the poet away from self-consciousness; "I" appears only in the references to time in the opening verse paragraphs.

The shift from the Lunch Poems' "strolling" poet who pauses at a "sample Olivetti" to the poet who "ponders" over the "eternal questions of life, co-existence and depth" occurs immediately after the announcement of the exact time in "A Step Away From Them." The artificial light of "neon" in daylight accentuates a darkness present even at noontime, as awareness of the transience of the lunch break initiates the reflection on mortality. This shift from natural light to neon is repeated with the association of "JULIET'S CORNER" with "Giulietta Masina," the Italian actress married to Federico Fellini (CP, 258). The movies provide the nighttime light with their "heavenly dimensions and reverberations and iconoclasms" ("To the Film Industry in Crisis," in CP, 232) to escape from the darkness of self-consciousness, especially from the consciousness of mortality. This preoccupation with death embedded in the structure of the lunch break becomes most apparent in the subsequent transition from present impressions to memory. Reflecting on the deaths of friends who were also public figures—Bunny Lang, John Latouche, Jackson Pollock—O'Hara fuses private memory with commemoration of artists, especially Pollock, who were commonly portrayed as tragic "victims" of the cold-war demands placed on artists. O'Hara momentarily takes a "step away" from his own autobiographical stance, replacing "I" with an impersonal, typical "one":

>   And one has eaten and one walks,
>   past the magazines with nudes

and the posters for BULLFIGHT and
the Manhattan Storage Warehouse,
which they'll soon tear down. I
used to think they had the Armory
Show there.

(CP, 258)

In replacing "I" with a reified self as past other, O'Hara situates his own act of commemorating avant-gardist figures in an irretrievable past. This act of momentary self-destruction replicates the response to imminent apocalypse that O'Hara saw animating Pollock's painting, but it also evokes Pollock's violent death. The violence of Pollock's painting reflects a repressed subtext of postwar American culture, and the poem questions how the act of internalizing this violence can be an effective mode for counteracting it. The poem then proceeds to implicate this sense of imminent destruction as an ongoing condition of American modernization; the "Manhattan Storage Warehouse / which they'll soon tear down" is associated with images linking the reified body with ritual violence, "the magazines with nudes / and the posters for BULLFIGHT" (CP, 258). Finally, the release from morbid self-consciousness, from the reflection on mortality, occurs through the poet's oblique affiliation with the historical avant-garde. This act of affiliation stresses the role of memory for reading the present, as the isolated "I" misconstrues the location of the event that marked the arrival of the European avant-garde in New York: the Armory Show. As in "Memorial Day 1950," "A Step Away From Them" appropriates historical narratives to structure personal memory, but personal memory in turn capriciously subverts the authority of historical narratives. And as in "The Day Lady Died" and "Personal Poem," the "post-anti-esthetic" surface of "A Step Away From Them" steps away from morbid self-consciousness not only through immersion in the overdetermined present but through reflection and reconstruction of the cultural and historical patterns that inform the moment.

O'Hara's "step away" from the self-destructiveness of Pollock indicates a reevaluation of how art should respond to the conditions of cold-war American culture. Yet his own "post-anti-esthetic" poetry certainly shares the same anxious relation to tradition that Harold Rosenberg's synopsis of Action Painting describes:

To come into being such a painting draws on the methods and vocabulary of existing art; in the process of production it invokes, positively and negatively, choices and references of painting; upon completion it is prized within the category of painting value and "hangs on the wall." In sum its being a work of art contradicts its being an action. . . . It retains its vigor as long as it continues to sustain its dilemmas: if it slips over into action ("life") there is no painting; if it is satisfied with itself as painting, it turns into "apocalyptic wallpaper."[30]

Like O'Hara's account of Pollock, Rosenberg's formulation of Action Painting is instructive for reading O'Hara's place in the "tradition of the new." O'Hara's poetry "sustains its dilemmas" through its attention to local, quotidian detail combined with self-consciousness about the aesthetic act of such attention. This self-consciousness about "appropriating" literary "choices and references" also can be paralyzing, however, as the tension between being "so damned literary" and "so damned empty" in "Poem en Forme de Saw" (*CP*, 429) most blatantly reveals. This tension informs all of O'Hara's poetry, but when it is structurally integrated to foreground the social subtexts informing interpretation, his "post-anti-esthetic" poetry enacts a crucial "revaluation" of modern literary history.

Instead of the specific intertexts invoked by his earlier pastiches and parodies, O'Hara's "lunch poems" foreground the New York cultural text in which modernism is disseminated, both in the institutionalization of "high art" and in mass culture. The temporal structure of the lunch break itself dramatizes the sense of exhausted urgency informing the "quandariness" of selection: the lunch break positions the poet within, but liminally outside, the restrictions of the employer's time clock, and the employer, the Museum of Modern Art, of course epitomizes the institutionalization of modern art in postwar America. Yet the lunch break also evokes the circular structure of what Harold Bloom has called the romantic "crisis-poem." In accentuating the disjunctions of his autobiographical reflections with romantic and modernist constructions of subjectivity and landscape, O'Hara's lunch poems exhibit not so much "anxiety of influence" as a "revaluation" of lyric subjectivity, a revaluation that foregrounds the postmodern reception of "tradition." As he claims in "Nature and New Painting," "nature" cannot be distinguished from "human nature" in O'Hara's modern urban landscape: "In past times there was nature and there was human nature; because of the ferocity of modern life, man and nature have become one."[31] The description of the local in an urban setting therefore always leads to consideration of the modes of signification that define the landscape. Similarly, the circular structure of O'Hara's lunch poems cannot be distinguished from the structure of the lunch break itself. Just as the urban landscape is a product of signification, the lunch break is a product of the work schedule. The urban scene does provoke meditation in these poems, but it is rarely depicted symbolically; significance is immanent in the names of people, places, and events. By adapting the circular pattern to the lunch break, and by transforming that pattern by attention to quotidian urban details, O'Hara interrogates the subject-object relations constructed in the romantic lyric. And by furthering the formal and linguistic experimentation of Williams's use of the vernacular, O'Hara "revaluates" the romantic definition of the local both geographically and linguistically. In doing so he underscores the romantic impulse of Williams's desire to merge subject and object, while recuperating the formal and linguistic experimentation that revealed the impossibility of such a "marriage." O'Hara simultaneously renews and deconstructs the romantic lyric; the dissonance resulting from this project arises from his postmodernist questioning of the expectations such a form raises.

The "I" that perceives the urban landscape in O'Hara's poetry is more a composite of multiple subject positions, the site of associations with the names of friends, places, and objects portrayed, than a coherent presence that stands apart to comment on them. His poetry rehearses the paradox of modern urban subjectivity explained by the sociologist Georg Simmel in an influential early twentieth-century essay:

> On the one hand, life is made infinitely easy for the personality in that stimulation, interests, uses of time and consciousness are offered to it from all sides. They carry the person as if in a stream, and one needs hardly to swim for oneself. On the other hand, however, life is composed more and more of these impersonal contents and offerings which tend to displace the genuine personal colorations and incomparabilities. This results in the individual summoning the utmost in uniqueness and particularization, in order to preserve his most personal core.[32]

The romantic "I" becomes divided in O'Hara's poems between what Simmel calls the "metropolitan blasé attitude"—the blunting of discriminations between the meanings and values of things that results from the money economy and from the "intensification of nervous stimulation"— and the compensatory exaggerated personality.[33] The dialectic between impersonality and personality, between "I" as object and "I" as subject, operates throughout O'Hara's poetry. He transforms the opposition between subject and world by treating his self as an object, but an object invested with personality, the "abstraction" opposed to the "abstract removal" of self in "Personism." Thus, O'Hara's personality, in all its dramatic multiplicity, becomes something that "still makes a poem a surprise." Part of the urban landscape, of the observed world, the poet's subject positions are likewise inseparable from the social fabric of this landscape. With the "stream of events / going so fast and the movingly / alternating with the amusingly" ("Post the Lake Poets Ballad," in *CP*, 336–37), the romantic dialectic of the "I" with the landscape becomes transformed into a kaleidoscopic colloquy of subject positions.

Frank O'Hara's "I do this I do that" poems subvert the very distinctions that he posits in "Post the Lake Poets Ballad." The poet who self-consciously "pretends to / be hurt" and the poet carried along by the "stream of events" continually collide and converge with each other in a pattern of the "movingly / alternating with the amusingly." Neither the "pretending" poetic voice nor the "stream of events" predominates; the poems constantly remind us that the subject both constructs and is constructed by the "stream of events." By foregrounding how the poetic enunciation is always situated, O'Hara's poetry is not restricted to the "merely" personal; rather, this poetry is continually opened to the historical and ideological forces that inform the "personal" at every moment.

6

"Words we have learned not to look at": George Oppen and Cold-War American Culture

It is difficult now to speak of poetry.
—George Oppen, "Of Being Numerous"

It is difficult now to speak of the New American Poetry as *the* American avant-garde tradition, or even as *the* "Williams tradition." The revival of the objectivists from their pre-1960s obscurity complicates any reductive overview that maps postwar American poetry exclusively in terms of the "war-games of the Beats and the Academics."[1] Ron Silliman has even attributed the extremism of the New American Poetry, in both form and content, to the supposed absence of any American literary avant-garde since the 1920s.[2] The extremity of this experimentation is itself symptomatic of the perceived distance it attempts to bridge between the generation of Pound and Williams and themselves. George Oppen's return to writing poetry after a twenty-five-year silence upsets such assumptions and represents a "third-phase objectivism," which, if not a renewed literary movement, was a return of the objectivist poets and poetics to the public eye. This return compels a reexamination of both the objectivist movement of the 1930s (the first phase) and its subsequent postwar absence from literary history (the second phase). Oppen's prolific poetic production in the 1960s and 1970s, prolific in the depth and complexity of its meditation on twentieth-century history, if not in its overall volume, has provoked not only a reconsideration of his peculiar position in the history of twentieth-century American poetry but of the reductive terms often used to define this history.

Oppen was himself self-conscious about, if not suspicious of, his reception by younger poets. In 1959, a quarter century after the publication of his first and then only published volume of poems, *Discrete Series* (1934)—a quarter century of literary silence that included labor organizing within the Communist Party during the Depression, combat in World War II, and political exile in Mexico during and after the McCarthy era—Oppen pondered over the possible response to the poetry he was in the process of writing. He wondered especially how younger poets would react to such topics as "the Infantry, skilled workers, row boats, people in trailer camps, the unemployed movement in the thirties, a family, marital love, children, the old codgers of Southern California, the H Bomb," as he writes in a 1959 letter to his sister and publisher, June Oppen Degnan:

> What in God's name will they make of it? And why will they like it? I have twenty-five years of life to write out, though, and that is what I'm going to do. I cannot cannot write . . . about "a world I never made" as every young poet that I know of is. I suspect I identify myself to them as the enemy the moment I accept some responsibility for the way things are—
> or: I'm thinking with some courage, and writing with some courage about a life which has had some courage, and which will end at least with the courage to acknowledge that I have had ancestors and will have descendents.[3]

Oppen's return to writing poetry was very much a return to his beginnings as an objectivist poet, but a return mediated by the historical consciousness impressed by his experience as a participant in those events that defined cold-war American culture. It is not surprising, then, that the writing he undertook upon returning to the United States is preoccupied with questions of birth and rebirth, of invention and renewal, of generation and succession. And of the "ancestors" to *his* "new American poetry," Williams's presence is the most pronounced. Oppen's return to writing is also marked by a reconsideration of Williams's Americanist avant-garde stance, especially given the terms of his emergent canonization.

Many of Oppen's readers have noted how his language, syntax, and prosody differs from Williams's.[4] Oppen's formal differences from Williams can be attributed to his poetry's greater concern with epistemological questions, his questioning the ways in which the subject perceives the object, and more specifically, the ways in which language mediates perception, compared to Williams's more empiricist mode of presenting the object. Williams's poems tend to proceed from image to related image, while Oppen's juxtaposed fragments tend to be conceptual rather than sensual. And if Williams's metric of action creates a "field of force in which the presence of the moment is made manifest," Oppen's "discrete series" of lines are more disjunctive, discriminatory, abrupt, a "movement of fits and starts."[5] Such assertions about representation that differentiate their poetics tend to focus on objects from the natural world, rather than from the social world, as their evidence. I would like to concentrate on the politics of representation in Williams and Oppen, to examine how Oppen's poetry of the 1960s revises Williams's populist stance, while reconsidering the impasse between leftist politics and avant-gardist poetics that compelled Oppen's earlier decision to stop writing poetry. Oppen's poetry offers no easy solutions to the apparently contradictory epistemology that informs his poetics—that while consciousness is inherently social, or intersubjective, there are limitations in one's mind and in language that restrict how much of the larger world one can honestly grasp.[6] Whether Oppen resolves the contradiction between his political and aesthetic commitments is less important than how he variously addresses the implications of this contradiction.[7] This contradiction is crucial to Oppen's dialogue with Williams's poetics, a dialogue most pronounced in the two volumes that inaugurated Oppen's return to poetry: *The Materials* (1962) and *This In Which* (1965). Oppen's revision of Williams's "populist" poetics demonstrates that the movement of "fits and charts" that characterizes his poetry is not simply an epistemological or formal question, but also a question of how one can know and represent the past, and more specifically, a question of how the disjunctions of violent historical change inform the perceived moment.

The initial poem in *The Materials* perhaps best demonstrates not only Oppen's preoccupation with questions of invention and renewal, and questions of historical continuity and discontinuity, but also his interest in the formation of Williams's postwar reputation. This poem, simply entitled "Eclogue," suggests what kind of poetic stance can respond critically to a historical moment of increased anxiety about potential nuclear war. By its title alone this poem announces its position in the pastoral tradition, even though the dialogue of this eclogue takes place not *within* a pastoral world, but *between* a pastoral world and those invested with the power to destroy it. The poem begins with the simple declaration: "The men talking/ Near the room's center" (*CP*, 17). But this conversation quickly turns more ominous: "They have said / More than they had intended" (*CP*, 17). Their conversation is one of strife, yet their disagreement threatens not so much those within the room as those outside their conversation:

> Pinpointing in the uproar
> of the living room
>
> An assault
> On the quiet continent.
>
> (*CP*, 17)

This "assault" is then juxtaposed to what is "Beyond the window":

> Tilting of itself to the sun once more, small
> Vegetative leaves
> And stems taking place
>
> Outside—O small ones,
> To be born!
>
> (*CP*, 17)

This conclusion not only quietly inverts the apocalyptic modernism of Yeats's conclusion to "The Second Coming," but echoes Williams's affirmation of rebirth in "Spring and All." By reiterating Williams's conclusion to what is often considered his rejoinder to "The Waste Land," Oppen foregrounds the similarity of Williams's "contagious hospital" to the rooms of the power brokers of his time, whose power to transform the landscape into a literal "wasteland" and whose power to impose such a mental landscape on their subjects are explored more directly in poems such as "The Crowded Countries of the Bomb" and "Time of the Missile." At the same time, Oppen humbly affirms the continuity of his poetics with Williams's early poetics, suggesting that invention, and thus destruction of that which is outmoded, is less important than recognizing continuity. In asserting an alternative to the technocratic idea of progress that had led to the brink of nuclear war, the intertextual dialogue provoked by "Eclogue" proposes a dialogic, intersubjective model of communication, one that can respect difference while affirming solidarity across time, a model opposing the hostile "dialogue" the poem initially presents.

In his review of *Discrete Series* Williams praised Oppen's "technical excellence," a quality that, he argues, sounds "unpoetic" but explains that "if an intelligence be deeply concerned with the bringing up of the body of poetry to a contemporary level equal with excellence of other times, technique means everything."[8] Oppen would not have disagreed with Williams's emphasis on the role of literary form for changing consciousness, which supports his distinction between poetry and propaganda, and which largely reiterates Louis Zukofsky's formulations of the poem as "object." However, Williams's conception of "objectivism" differs from Oppen's quite consistently. For example, Williams's version of literary history in his *Autobiography* has as much to say about the paradox of the avant-garde "tradition" as any of his subsequent critics have had to say. Williams describes how objectivism was "inaugurated" in response to the limitations of imagism, which had "dribbled off into 'free verse'":

> There is no such thing as free verse! Verse is measure of some sort. "Free verse" was without measure and needed none for its projected objectifications. Thus the poem had run down and become formally non extant.
>
> But, we argued, the poem, like every other form of art, is an object, an object that in itself formally presents its case and its meaning by the very form it assumes. Therefore, being an object, it should be so treated and controlled—but not as in the past. For past objects have about them past necessities—like the sonnet—which have conditioned them and from which, as a form itself, they cannot be freed.
>
> The poem being an object (like a symphony or cubist painting) it must be the purpose of the poet to make of his words a new form: to invent, that is, an object consonant with his day. This was what we wished to imply by Objectivism, an antidote, in a sense, to the bare image haphazardly presented in loose verse. (*A*, 264–65)

Most remarkable in this summary of objectivist theory is Williams's defensiveness about the notion of "form," as he distinguishes the objectivist notion of form from the traditional notion of genre. The unanswered question of course is whether the objectivist poem in itself could ultimately acquire such "necessities" as other "past objects."

Williams's insistence on invention, the poet's act of making, differs from both Zukofsky's and Oppen's interpretations of the poet's role in incorporating "historic and contemporary particulars"[9] into the objectivist poem. Oppen, like Zukofsky, stresses the ethics of the poet's stance toward his subject matter, as he emphasizes how the poem should convey the poet's "sincerity." Concerned less with the poem's implicitly antagonistic stance toward his audience, Oppen instead proposes a less egocentric stance toward the world, as his retrospective definition of "objectivism" shows: "What I felt I was doing was beginning from imagism as a position of honesty. The first question at that time in poetry was simply the question of honesty, of sincerity. But I learned from Louis, as against the romanticism or even the quaintness of the imagist position, the necessity for forming a poem properly, for achieving form. That's what 'objectivist' really means."[10] Such a stance assumes a mode of reading that recreates the poet's act of encounter, of discovery, through the poem's formal devices. What Williams, Zukofsky, and Oppen share is a disdain for a rhetorical use of the image that displays the poet's mastery over the object for the reader's passive consumption. Oppen in fact departed from Zukofsky in his impatience with his obscurity, or "secretiveness."[11] What distinguishes Oppen from both Williams and Zukofsky is the extent to which he invites, indeed compels, his readers to reflect on how language, on the simplest levels of syntax, mediates perception.

Oppen takes up Williams's question of invention most directly in the first poem he wrote upon returning to writing, "Blood from the Stone." This complex reflection on the role of poetry in times of violent upheaval is at once an autobiographical reflection on those experiences most crucial to Oppen's life and a meditation on constructions of time. After declaring the powerful bond of marriage that has transcended the experience of violent historical change in Oppen's life—"Everything I am is/ Us. Come home" (*CP*, 31)—the poem reflects on the lasting determining presence of the past:

> The Thirties. And
> A spectre
>
> In every street,
> In all inexplicable crowds, what they did then
> Is still their lives.

> (*CP*, 31)

"Their lives" of course includes the lives of George and Mary Oppen, which the poem self-consciously goes on to consider:

> As thirty in a group—
> To Home Relief—the unemployed—

> Within the city's intricacies
> Are these lives. Belief?
> What do we believe
> To live with? Answer.
> Not invent—just answer—all
> That verse attempts.
> That we can somehow add each to each other?
>
> —Still our lives.
>
> (*CP*, 31)

Within the syntactic "intricacies" of these lines is the revision of Williams's dictum to "invent . . . an object consonant with his day." The response to the question of "belief" epitomizes Oppen's inventive technique of breaking lines to heighten syntactic ambiguity. "What do we believe" appears to be at first a reiteration of the question raised in the previous line, but this question is simultaneously complicated and answered with its completion in the next line. "What do we believe / To live with?" is an unusual construction that foregrounds the material contingency of belief, that is, its inextricable relation to everyday life. At the same time, "To live with" accentuates the social nature of "belief." "Belief" is that which we "believe" we "live with," i.e., that which supports our everyday decisions, yet only the act of "living with," reiterating the initial stanza's assertion ("Everything I am is / Us."), validates what "we believe." The rhyme of "Belief" with "relief" and the near rhyme of "believe" with "lives" and "live" further accentuates the intricate relations of "belief" to social life. The subsequent lines are similarly ambiguous, although less so syntactically. The simple one-word response to the question of belief, "Answer," affirms the significance of response in itself, which is an act of faith that motivates the poem. As verb and noun, act and deed, "Answer" engages its readers in conversation, a process heightened by its repetition in the following line. This repetition of "answer," which is offered as an alternative to Williams's avant-gardist insistence on invention, registers doubly here, but its adverbial sense of diminishment—namely, "only answer"—does not entirely erase its adjectival sense of an ethical imperative. If the act of responding to such fundamental questions as "belief" does not in itself make an answer "just," the conversation compelled by such syntactic ambiguity does indeed justify what appear to be diminished expectations for verse. The expectations Oppen suggests in his return to writing poetry are nothing less than the establishment of grounds for community, or the grounds for representing difference within communities through the interrogation of syntactic patterns of relation.

"Blood from the Stone" goes on to question the impact that World War II had had on the poet and, more specifically, on the subsequent possibility for a traditional lyric stance:

> There is a simple ego in a lyric,
> A strange one in war.
> To a body anything can happen,
> Like a brick. Too obvious to say.
> But all horror came from it.
>
> (CP, 32)

Such a transformed notion of community that participation in warfare compels, one that heightens both the awareness of mortal solitude and of how this solitude is shared, cannot simply be left behind. The final section of the poem considers the role of memory for understanding the multiple nature of time. It stresses the strength of social bonds that characterize everyday life, as well as those that mask historical continuity from generation to generation:

> Fifty years
> Sidereal time
> Together, and among the others,
> The bequeathed pavements, the inherited lit streets:
> Among them we were lucky—strangest word.
>
> (CP, 33)

It then relates this historical sense of time, the living past "bequeathed" or "inherited" from prior generations, which is remembered, or construed, as historical continuity within geological time, the "planet's / Time," which has an unexpected immediacy,

> because we find the others
> Deserted like ourselves and therefore brothers. Yet
>
> So we lived
> and chose to live
>
> These were our times.
>
> (CP, 33)

"Our times" are multiple—not just intellectual conceptions of the times the poem variously construes but the lived times shared by husband and wife, by the poet and his various communities. "These" times are also both past and present; they are present in their pastness but also present as the results of decisions made, actions taken. But ultimately the poem asserts the commonality of "others / Deserted . . . therefore brothers," an inclusive commonality extended beyond marriage and other intimate social bonds.

The commonality asserted at the end of "Blood from the Stone" results from, yet supersedes, the questions provoked by the Depression and World War II. This commonality is compelled by the "historical and contemporary particulars" of "our times," the technological capability to indeed alter the planet's time, the "nuclear capability" that makes us "endangered / Totally at last" ("Time of the Missile," in *CP*, 49). Such a compelled commonality certainly challenges the conventional stance of the lyric "ego," as well as the avant-gardist compulsion to "invent." This "time of the missile" furthermore questions conventional definitions of agency, diminishing the poet's power to "invent . . . an object consonant with his day," unless of course this threat to agency is itself dramatized in the structure of the poem, as "The Crowded Countries of the Bomb" perhaps best demonstrates.

The lyric "I" never appears in "The Crowded Countries of the Bomb," for the questions it raises transcend individual decisions, as they threaten the very capability for choice. Yet at the same time its ambiguous mode of questioning makes choice unavoidable:

> What man could do,
> And could not
> And chance which has spared us
> Choice, which has shielded us
>
> As if a god.

(CP, 57)

The initial clause of this poem itself raises the question of individual responsibility for one's actions. "What man" could refer to an individual—"which man"—while "man" also evokes "mankind"; given the enormous responsibility invested in those with power to deploy "the bomb," one man's decision could indeed affect all of humanity. This

conditional clause further questions the grounds for action: "What man
could do" implies both the capability for action and the capability for
choosing to act. The question of "what man could do" is hardly resolved in the conclusion of this "sentence"; the lack of syntactic closure
accentuates both the enormous implications of acting "as if a god" and
the concurrent imperative to recognize this power and to choose to
resist its numbing effects. The absence of an active verb to conclude the
second line, "And could not," suggests both the utter, final unspeak-
ability of "what man could do" and the failure to confront this possibility. The paratactic syntax of these lines furthermore suggests a failure
to rationally connect the ability to act (or not act) with the implications
of action (or passivity), thus making "chance" both actor and action,
noun and verb. The line break after "chance which has spared us" reiterates the double imperative to recognize and to act. If one accepts that
only "chance" has "spared us / Choice," then one accepts that only
"chance . . . has spared us." Such blind acquiescence to cold-war rhetoric overlooks the political decisions that led to such a dependence on
"chance." The indeterminate referent of the dependent clause, "which
has shielded us / As if a god" (is it "choice," "chance," or "what man
could do . . . which has shielded us"?), similarly stresses both the hubris
of those with the power to act "as if a god" and the apparent powerless-
ness of those who passively acquiesce to such power.

"The Crowded Countries of the Bomb" questions how we come to
terms with the prospect of nuclear holocaust:

> What is the name of that place
> We have entered:
> Despair? Ourselves?
>
> (CP, 57)

Yet even such a commonplace word as "ourselves" has unprecedented
implications. To what can "ourselves" be opposed when "we can destroy ourselves / Now"? "Ourselves" cannot be easily differentiated
from other selves when "ourselves" are already other, just as "Now"—
accentuated by its position in the line alone—is itself other, magnified
in its ephemerality and yet diminished by the consciousness of the cause
for its magnified ephemerality. Yet the poem does not ultimately rest
with this sense of "despair":

> Walking in the shelter,
> The young and the old,
> Of each other's backs and shoulders
>
> Entering the country that is
> Impenetrably ours.

(CP, 57)

Although the nation can indeed be seen as a bomb shelter during the late 1950s and early 1960s, "The Crowded Countries of the Bomb" nonetheless affirms a faith in the people who temporarily inhabit this "country" among other "countries." The contradiction that this conclusion poses, furthermore, reiterates the poem's rejection of "despair." "Impenetrably ours" implies both that which is intellectually incomprehensible and that which is physically inaccessible, but the collective act of "entering" this impenetrable "country" suggests otherwise. Perhaps more apropos to a poem concerned with the psychological impact of living with the bomb is the meaning of *impenetrability* in physics, i.e., the property of matter whereby two bodies cannot occupy the same space simultaneously. By insisting that the prospect of nuclear holocaust forces us to understand that *all* bodies occupy the same place simultaneously, the poem challenges the us/them mentality of cold-war culture. And by compelling his readers to constantly consider multiple interpretations simultaneously, interpretations that do not easily coalesce into a comprehensive closure, Oppen furthermore subverts such polar thinking.

Oppen's writing conveys a continuity with Williams's poetics ("Eclogue"), a similarity that crosses the historical gap of his "silence," but it also foregrounds the discontinuity within continuity, or the continuity of discontinuity ("Blood from the Stone"), the difference that acknowledges the demands of the postmodernist historical moment defined by "The Crowded Countries of the Bomb." In his reading of other writers whose poetry was similarly engaged with the American avant-garde tradition, especially the Black Mountain poets, Oppen is quite clear about the poet's responsibility toward both literary tradition and the historical moment. For example, he criticizes Olson for his "surprising susceptibility to influence," especially to the pervasive influence of Pound. He argues that "if we look to poetry as a skill by which we can grasp the form of a perception achieved," then "to encounter Olson's work, in spite of the currency of the phrase, is simply not an encounter with a new poetry. The question finally becomes not only how new is the voice, but how fresh therefore is the vision, and with it the materials of which the poetry makes use or which it has available to it."[12] Oppen objects to this mimicry of Pound's voice not because Olson fails to openly acknowledge his appropriation, but because Pound's overwhelming presence causes one to doubt the "sincerity" of Olson's vision. Consequently, the "materials" of Olson's poetry cannot be conveyed in a "fresh" form, one responsive to the "historic particulars" that differentiate his world from Pound's. Rachel Blau DuPlessis has explained how Oppen rewrites Pound's poetics, especially given the authoritarian political implications of what Oppen called "Pound's ego system, Pound's organization of the world around a character, a kind of masculine energy."[13] Oppen's revision of Williams's poetics is more subtle, because Williams's "populist" vision was more amenable to Oppen's politics, but his assessment of Williams is similarly sensitive to the transmission and transformation of poetic stances from one generation to the next. In his only published essay, "The Mind's Own Place," Oppen takes up the question of Williams's influence on the "new American poets," concentrating on the significance of Williams's populist stance in its own time and for the early 1960s. This essay was, as Oppen explains, addressed to Denise Levertov, who was then the poetry editor of the *Nation* and who was beginning to write more openly declamatory political poems, poems of which Oppen disapproved.[14] In differentiating his principles from those of other postwar poets, this essay thus has much to say about the politics of *his* political stance.

In "The Mind's Own Place" Oppen defines Williams's significance for twentieth-century poetry, especially for the "Beat" poetry gaining the most notoriety at the time of this essay (1963). At the same time he redefines the politics of Williams's Americanist poetics, articulating especially his own revision of Williams's predominant mode of representing working-class subjects. Oppen positions Williams as the most notable modernist poet whose writing could be broadly labeled "populist." Allying Williams's early modernist sensibility with that of such poets as Alfred Kreymborg, Vachel Lindsay, and Carl Sandburg, Oppen writes that "of the major poets" only "Williams, with his insistence on 'the American idiom,' on the image derived from day to day experience, on form as 'nothing more than an extension of content,' . . . shows a derivation from populism." He distinguishes "the fidelity, the clarity, including the visual clarity and their freedom from the art subject" that differentiate Williams, Pound, and Eliot from the "romanticism, the mere sentimental 'going on' of such men as Sandburg and Kreymbourg," while at the same time defining *his* formulation of objectivist poetics, the inheritance from imagism that characterizes Williams's best poetry: "It is possible to find a metaphor for anything, an analogue: but the image is encountered, not found; it is an account of the poet's perception, of the act of perception; it is a test of sincerity, a test of conviction, the rare poetic quality of truthfulness."[15] Williams's poetry exemplifies what "modernism restored to poetry, the sense of the poet's self among things. So much depends on the red wheelbarrow."[16] Yet if so much depends upon Williams's red wheelbarrow for a retrospective account of modernism, this same image epitomizes how the institutionalization of modernism, and specifically the canonization of Williams, had diminished the impact that such an image can have on subsequent audiences. Commenting on the generally unfavorable reception of William Bronk's poetry, Oppen elsewhere writes that "there seemed in the late twenties something childish about writing of red wheel barrows, rather than the more stately mansions of the soul. Apparently there seems something childish now about writing of anything else."[17] The "red wheelbarrow" itself becomes a cliché when substituted for "a test of sincerity, a test of conviction." So much depends upon the historical context of the red wheelbarrow's reception.

What ultimately governs Williams's impact on those poets writing against the grain of the "Academics" is his populism. Yet the question of Williams's populism also marks Oppen's primary point of departure from his politics and poetics. In "The Mind's Own Place" he writes that "if the word *populism* applied to Williams may not be altogether justifiable, it is at any rate true that Williams is the most American of the American poets of his generation, and these young poets have been markedly and as a matter of course American."[18] Oppen's contrast of *populist* with *American* here provokes the essay's inquiry into the relation of the politics of class to the politics of nationality, as well as the relation of politics to poetry more generally. This contrast of *populist* with *American* suggests Williams's appeal to Oppen, but it also marks his dissent from Williams's poetics, a dissent also from the predominant appropriation of Williams's poetics by the New American Poets. What admirably links the New American Poets with their "populist" literary predecessors is a "search for the common experience, for the ground under their feet." And this search does have a potential political effect on its audience: "The poet means to trust to his direct perceptions, and it is even possible that it might be useful for the country to listen, to hear evidence, to consider what indeed we have brought forth upon this continent."[19] Yet such an emphasis on the American experience, which Oppen sees primarily in terms of the experience of immigration, justifies neither a narrowly nationalistic definition of ethics nor a nationalistic definition of the poet's stance; if the Adamic stance so prevalent in American lyric poetry is delusive, then so is the twentieth-century Whitmanian poet's nationalistic appeal to the commonality of Americans.

A poem from *This In Which*, "Street," illustrates Oppen's critique of the sort of populism most frequently associated with Williams. Like a number of Oppen's poems, "Street" echoes Williams's objectivist lyrics, in this case most explicitly a poem such as "The Poor," although its intertextual evocation of Williams is more overtly parodic, more critical, than his quotations tend to be. Whereas "The Poor" begins with a picturesque description that explains why "It's the anarchy of poverty / delights me" (*CP 1*, 453), "Street" disavows such aesthetic pleasure, as it begins:

> Ah these are the poor
> These are the poor—
>
> Bergen street.
>
> (*CP*, 109)

Williams's poem describes the working-class neighborhood; the "anarchy of poverty" is portrayed through one representative urban scene described in careful detail. Oppen's poem utterly avoids such description, such portrayal, explaining instead in stark terms—"Humiliation, / Hardship . . ." (*CP*, 109)—the cruel ordeal of poverty. The conclusion of "The Poor" further exemplifies Williams's tendency to individualize the effects of poverty:

> the old man
> in a sweater and soft black
> hat who sweeps the sidewalk—

> his own ten feet of it
> in a wind that fitfully
> turning his corner has
> overwhelmed the entire city.
>
> (*CP 1*, 453)

Williams's "old man," like other figures of his "proletarian portraits," is heroic in his proud care for his ten feet of sidewalk, but such heroism is ultimately futile in the face of the overwhelming force over which he has no control. Although the conclusion rejects the ideology of bourgeois individualism, the poem's exclusive focus on the specific effects of poverty obscures its systematic roots, figured here by the natural force of the wind. By affirming the bourgeois gesture of caring for one's ten feet of property, even in the face of apocalypse, the poem not only affirms the ideology that informs this gesture but takes a condescending stance toward the poor who are subjected by this ideology.

Williams tried throughout the 1930s to reconcile leftist political demands with his descriptive poetry, as Robert von Hallberg has explained.[20] Although he had occasionally practiced and had never totally disavowed explanatory or declamatory poetry, his defense of descriptive poetry became more vigorous in response to Marxist critics who criticized the neutral stance of the objectivists. Williams followed Zukofsky in defending analytical description, as opposed to appreciative description, against claims that descriptive poetry was neutral, impersonal, and nonpartisan. A poem like "The Poor" exemplifies how the subjects portrayed in Williams's 1930s poetry themselves invite political interpretations of his descriptive writing. Oppen's "Street" represents one such interpretation, especially in its conclusion, as it sustains its refusal to represent "the poor" in images that aestheticize, or implicitly glorify, their condition.

"Street" concludes with a telling look to the disillusionment produced by poverty, which in turn evokes the 1930s figured in Williams's proletarian portraits:

> And this is real pain,
> Moreover. It is terrible to see the children,
>
> The righteous little girls;
> So good, they expect to be so good . . .
>
> (*CP*, 109)

Hardly subtle in its echo, the repetition of "so good" evokes Williams's "poor old woman," "munching a plum on / the street" (*CP 1*, 383). The sensual portrayal of the woman—"Comforted / a solace of ripe plums" that "taste good to her"—celebrates a moment of relief from despair. "Street," in contrast, offers no relief, no "solace," no comforting images by which to identify with "the poor." Oppen instead simply conveys the "terrible" fact of diminished expectations, of ultimate hopelessness, that awaits the "righteous little girls." Such an allusive contrast challenges the primitivist assumptions that inform Williams's descriptive poems, whether celebrating the working-class kitsch of "The Poor" or the sensual physicality of working-class types in "To a Poor Old Woman."

Oppen certainly had no illusions about the political effects of his poetry. In his interview with L. S. Dembo he reiterates the distinction between poetry and political action he articulates in "The Mind's Own Place": "If you decide to do something politically, you do something that has political efficacy. And if you decide to write poetry, then you write poetry, not something that you hope, or deceive yourself into believing, can save people who are suffering."[21] And although referring to the dilemma of the leftist poet in the 1930s, he later reiterates this position in terms more appropriate to the refusal to represent "the poor" in "Street." In a 1966 letter to his daughter, Linda Oppen Mourelatos, he writes: "I become so angry at those who depend on the poor, the oppressed, for their ethical well-being, for their 'values' . . . I wish the poor and the oppressed did not exist, and we could look only for what we really do value. . . . the thing begins with the positive, with what one does want."[22] Oppen here articulates the utopian view of poetry that informs a poetic stance that empathizes with "the oppressed," yet not to the extent of celebrating their condition. A brief poem entitled "From Disaster" perhaps best demonstrates this stance; it affirms the strength by which immigrants have overcome economic hardship, yet implicitly questions the socioeconomic system that sustains such disparities of wealth. More specifically, the poem questions the bourgeois value attached to property ownership as a goal in itself, which although effective as a motivational force is ultimately an unsatisfying substitute for a more meaningful notion of "home."

"From Disaster" draws an analogy between the poet's quest for form and the immigrant's quest for "home." The poem begins with a direct statement of poetic principle:

> Ultimately the air
> Is bare sunlight where must be found
> The lyric valuables.
>
> (CP, 29)

"From Disaster" paradoxically begins with the end, the "ultimate," the final principle as first principle. Yet this beginning denies a facile acceptance, and facile proclamation, of "ultimate" ontological principles, or of "lyric valuables" that transcend the poet's and reader's act of finding. The play on "found" is especially important here, for the "lyric valuables" may be discovered, preexisting, in "bare sunlight," or they may be originated by those who seek them; what matters is the act of finding, an act that the syntax suggests is an interplay of subject and object and is neither a wholly objective nor wholly subjective mode of discovery.

This imperative to find, or "found," the "lyric valuables" is itself grounded in the one-sentence narrative that follows, a narrative that concisely presents the legacy of the immigrant settlement of the New World:

> From disaster
>
> Shipwreck, whole families crawled
> To the tenements, and there
>
> Survived by what morality
> Of hope
>
> Which for the sons
> Ends its metaphysic
> In small lawns of home.
>
> (CP, 29)

The poem moves from "disaster," the conclusion of the first stanza, which itself begins in "the air," to "shipwreck," from metaphysical speculation on the "ultimate" to the desperate necessity of immigrants aground. Yet this movement of descent—"From disaster / Shipwreck"—descent not only in space but in time, the American descent from immigrants that the poem narrates, is subsequently inverted to one of ascent, the Darwinian notion of evolutionary ascent, of "crawling" from the ocean to "the tenements," and the ascent of immigrants who aspire to "upward mobility." Such a trajectory as this poem proposes does not straightforwardly assert either an unqualified admiration for such an ethic of survival in itself, nor an ironic criticism of such delusions propagated by the ideology of "the American dream." "Small lawns of home" is neither a utopian image nor an ironically denigrated image of the American "morality / Of hope." The poem raises more questions about the legacy of immigrant dreams than it answers. "By what morality / Of hope" can be taken as a question or an assertion; it expresses both incredulity and admiration for the transmission of immigrant values to "the sons." Yet does this "morality / Of hope . . . end" in the minds of the immigrants, hope for the sons, or does it end with the sons who "find" their "metaphysic" in "small lawns of home"? The "lyric valuables" lie less in the observed fact than in the social roots of the fact, just as the "small lawns of home" have less value in themselves than in the generations of hardship through which they were attained. "From Disaster" ultimately ends far from where it "ultimately" began, in the mundane "small lawns" of immigrant descendants. If such a conclusion seems to signify disappointment over the quest for "ultimate" answers, "From Disaster" does not end merely with the materialist denigration of the "morality / Of hope," or "of home," which closes the poem with the question of how family history and, less specifically, nationality constitute and continually reconstitute what we mean by "home."

The problematic of "home" is more explicitly located within American history in "The Building of the Skyscraper." Like "From Disaster," this poem succinctly articulates an open-form aesthetic that questions conventional grounds for a progressive national history. In doing so it questions the will to obliterate the past that implicates both avant-gardist aesthetic principles and socioeconomic policies of "urban renewal." The poem begins with the portrait of the poet as construction worker:

> The steel worker on the girder
> Learned not to look down, and does his work
> And there are words we have learned
> Not to look at,
> Not to look for substance
> Below them. But we are on the verge
> Of vertigo.
>
> (*CP*, 131)

This analogy of poet to steelworker questions whether the worker's refusal to "look down" is less an act of confident craftsmanship than a fearful repression of "vertigo." "We" for whom the poet speaks thus become blind to the assumptions that support the "words we have learned / Not to look at." The beginning of the second stanza articulates this repressed fear in syntax that is itself "on the verge / Of vertigo":

> There are words that mean nothing
> But there is something to mean.
>
> (*CP*, 131)

This seemingly circular statement responds to the challenge posed by the initial analogy, yet simultaneously enacts the sense of vertigo underlying the image of the steelworker on the girder. The line break of this statement suggests several interpretations. The first line forms an assertion in itself, but it implies both that there are words that are meaningless and words that express the meaning of nothingness. The qualifying conclusion of this assertion is similarly double: there are meaningless words that are insufficient for expressing what there is to mean, and there are words that convey the barely articulate urgency that there is something to mean. Or, to paraphrase this statement in Oppen's terms: "[T]he question is not of the meaning of a specific word, but of restoring *words* to meaning as, I do not think one could speak of restoring language to *its* meaning, but to meaning."[23]

"The Building of the Skyscraper" ultimately descends from its metaphysical heights to an image more reminiscent of Williams:

> O, the tree, growing from the sidewalk—
> It has a little life, sprouting
> Little green buds
> Into the culture of the streets.
>
> (*CP*, 131)

Yet it does not conclude with a sentimental portrait of "the culture of the streets." Its conclusion moves from the initial speculation about modernity to the specific historical conditions of American modernity, with the antihistorical impulse that makes consciousness of the past as threatening in its otherness as consciousness of the ground below the girder:

> We look back
> Three hundred years and see bare land.
> And suffer vertigo.
>
> (*CP*, 131)

Like "the steel worker on the girder" who "learned not to look down," "we" too have learned to ignore that which supports us, that which "lies" below the everyday words with which we habitually, unconsciously converse. Yet this conclusion suggests that we ignore "the culture of the streets" for fear of falling, that the image of "bare land" that mystifies American history simultaneously blinds us and supports us from the "substance" of the past. This conclusion to "The Building of the Skyscraper" is indeed a sweeping commentary on the "learned" myopic ignorance of history conveyed by the Adamic myth, which posits the origins of the American past in a tradition of "bare land" rather than in any "culture of the streets." And here the figure of the steelworker becomes more telling. He is a worker, certainly, and not implausibly a native American worker, whose contribution to the building of skyscrapers has itself been obscured from the dominant historical consciousness and whose elevated distance from the land below is certainly suggestive. Here the physical trajectory of the poem's beginning is conflated with the historical trajectory of its conclusion. The "vertigo" with which it closes conveys both an unsettling distance from the land, a distance that accentuates its otherness and also the beginning of an equally unsettling distance from the Americanist myth of the "bare land," a distance that the poem vertiginously stresses.

In her autobiography, *Meaning a Life*, Mary Oppen describes a moment of departure from the West Coast of her husband's and her youth, a moment that initiates their quest for a populist open-form poetic. Her recollection of hitchhiking across the country is especially apropos to her husband's mode of writing:

> We were in search of an esthetic within which to live, and we were looking for it in our own American roots, in our own country. We had learned at college that poetry was being written in our own times, and that in order for us to write it was not necessary for us to ground ourselves in the academic; the ground we needed was the roads we were travelling. As we were new, so we had new roots, and we knew little of our own country. Hitchhiking became more than flight from a powerful family—our discoveries themselves became an esthetic and a disclosure. The people we met, as various and as accidentally met as thumbing a ride could make them, became the clue to our finding roots; we gained confidence that this country was ours in a sense we hadn't known under our parents' roofs.[24]

Such stories of departure and arrival, of flight and discovery, of "finding roots" in the most unpredictable encounters, inform George Oppen's quest for a politically engaged, open-form poetics. In describing the prosodic method of his later poetry he reiterates this experience of the unexpected:

> It is true that my own temperament, my own sense of drama, enters into this: I like to seem to be speaking very simply—and a sense of drama is dangerous, I know that, this is again a question of modulation, as is music: a question of honesty, question of sincerity—the sincerity of the *I* and the *we*, it is tremendous drama, the things that common words say, the words "and" and "but" and "is" and "before" and "after." Our true faith is said in the simple words, for we cannot escape them—for meaning is the instant of meaning—and this means that we write to find what we believe and what we do not believe. . . .[25]

And what effects do poems that so stress the "words we have learned / not to look at" have on their readers? Oppen answers this question in less certain, but nonetheless suggestive, terms: "It is possible that they contribute only to the process which is stripping people of their defenses."[26] It is indeed possible that Oppen's allusive postwar writing represents a departure from what Fredric Jameson has called the "protopolitical vocation and the terrorist stance of the older modernism," but by prosodically and syntactically leaving readers "on the verge / of vertigo," compelling them to consider multiple interpretations simultaneously, interpretations that do not always coalesce into a conclusive sense of closure, this writing powerfully subverts the dominant us/them mentality of cold-war American culture.

Notes

CHAPTER 1. INTRODUCTION

1. Donald M. Allen, preface to *The New American Poetry* (New York: Grove, 1960), xi.

2. As Allen writes in his preface to *The New American Poetry*, "These poets have already created their own tradition, their own press, and their public" (xi). The question of how the New American Poetry continued or deviated from earlier avant-garde movements was hardly self-evident, even to its earliest critics, despite the ever-present comparisons with the anthology edited by Donald Hall, Robert Pack, and Louis Simpson, namely, *New Poets of England and America* (New York: New American Library, 1957). In her review of *The New American Poetry* for the *New Yorker*, Louise Bogan was representative of many poets of her generation in asking whether the anthology presented a new poetic or the antipoetic: "Is this a true avant-garde manifestation,—does it, that is, arise from a fresh, creative impulse centrally related to the present growing and changing needs of art in general and poetry in particular—or is it something else? Is it, for example, a late and peculiarly American development of the post-Symbolist revolt, which brought in, very nearly fifty years ago, dada and surrealism? Or is it the kind of revolt that has little to do with literature, ancient or modern?" Review of *The New American Poetry*, edited by Donald M. Allen, *New Yorker*, 8 October 1960, 199–200. Bogan questions nothing less than the very terms of the anthology's title: what is "new," "American," and "poetic" about *The New American Poetry*?

Poet-critics who promoted the New American Poetry stressed its renewal of the international avant-garde. For example, Kenneth Rexroth called it the "return to the mainstream of modern verse as it has been practised, throughout the world—except in England—for the past half century." "The New Poetry," in *Assays* (New York: New Directions, 1961), 185. David Antin would similarly distinguish between the "strongly anti-modernist and provincial" New Critical version of modernism and "the hybrid modernism of Pound, and the purer modernism of Gertrude Stein and William Carlos Williams." "Modernism and Postmodernism: Approaching the Present in American Poetry," *Boundary 2* 1 (1972): 120. Antin stresses the continuity of "collage modernism" and its "postmodernist" successors. Jerome Rothenberg's anthology *Revolution of the Word* similarly attempts to recuperate the "immediate pre-history" of the post–World War II avant-garde, as have subsequent Language poetry anthologies. See Rothenberg, "pre-face" to *Revolution of the Word: A Gathering of American Avant-Garde Poetry, 1914-1945* (New York: Seabury, 1974).

146

3. Alan C. Golding's analysis of the role poetry anthologies play in canon formation is especially useful for understanding this process. See "A History of American Poetry Anthologies," in *Canons*, ed. Robert von Hallberg (Chicago: University of Chicago Press, 1984), particularly 300-301, where he discusses the New American Poetry. The introductions to the successors to Allen's anthology—namely, *The Poetics of the New American Poetry* (1973) and *The Postmoderns: The New American Poetry Revised* (1982)—themselves indicate how the evolution of the New American Poetry concurs with Golding's analysis. In *The New American Poetry*, the "true continuers of the modern movement" are initially grouped geographically by the locales of their poetic "communities" or "schools." In *The Poetics of the New American Poetry*, this "avant-garde" is dispersed within a wider tradition of poets who share the desire for a "new or re-newed writing in hopes of a new or re-newed world," a tradition that descends from Whitman. Warren Tallman, preface to *The Poetics of the New American Poetry*, ed. Donald Allen and Warren Tallman (New York: Grove, 1973), xi. The repetition of "re-newed" along with "new" suggests that the "search for the new" entails a return to past traditions as much as a rejection of their restrictions. This sense of belatedness marks a retreat from Allen's more aggressive earlier stance. In *The Postmoderns* the New American Poetry is no longer an oppositional movement but the "dominant force in the American poetic tradition." Donald M. Allen, preface to *The Postmoderns: The New American Poetry Revised*, ed. Donald M. Allen and George F. Butterick (New York: Grove, 1982), 9. The emphasis on alternative presses and public reading networks is, in the introduction *The New American Poetry*, forsaken for the less politicized dichotomy of open-form and academic rhymed and metered poetry. Experimental poetry is described in nationalistic terms as the work of "the most truly authentic indigenous American writing" (9). The designation *postmodern*, which replaces the local affiliations that grouped the "new American poetry," is characterized by its "inclusiveness, its quick willingness to take advantage of all that had gone before" (9)—hardly the confrontational avant-gardist stance that made *The New American Poetry* so controversial.

4. The journals *Boundary 2*, *Paideuma*, *Sagetrieb*, and *William Carlos Williams Review* have been instrumental in redressing New Critical versions of modernism; they position the imagist and objectivist traditions more centrally within twentieth-century literary history. Critics whose works have been similarly influential in defining Williams's significance for postmodernism include Charles Altieri, David Antin, Burton Hatlen, Marjorie Perloff, Joseph N. Riddell, and William Spanos.

5. See Peter Schmidt, introduction to *William Carlos Williams, The Arts, and Literary Tradition* (Baton Rouge: Louisiana State University Press, 1988), esp. 4–6. These critical presuppositions inform the majority of the historical studies of Williams's career that were responsible for increased academic recognition of him in the 1970s; the exclusion of texts that subvert linear plots for his development assumes a New Critical hierarchy of genres and modes. See, for example, James E. B. Breslin, *William Carlos Williams: An American Artist* (New York: Oxford University Press, 1970); James Guimond, *The Art of William Carlos Williams: A Discovery and Possession of America* (Urbana: University of Illinois Press, 1968); and Thomas R. Whitaker, *William Carlos Williams* (Boston: Twayne, 1968). These books are all especially valuable for their readings of a range of Williams's writings. Many critical overviews have also taken a heroic form that charts Williams's career as a series of progressive "peaks" of artistic production. See Guimond, *Art of William Carlos Williams*, and Richard A. Macksey, " 'A Certainty of Music': Williams' Changes," in *William Carlos Williams: A Collection of Critical Essays*, ed. J. Hillis Miller (Englewood Cliffs, N.J.: Prentice-Hall, 1966), 132–47.

Even more prevalent are studies that trace his ascension through imagist and objectivist "phases" to the epic grandeur of *Paterson* and the "pure poetry" of the late lyrics. This pattern characterizes approaches to Williams's oeuvre such as J. Hillis Miller's phenomenological reading of his poetics, *Poets of Reality: Six Twentieth-Century Writers* (Cambridge: Belknap Press of Harvard University Press, 1966), 285–359; Joseph N. Riddel's poststructuralist reading, *The Inverted Bell: Modernism and the Counterpoetics of William Carlos Williams* (Baton Rouge: Louisiana State University Press, 1974), and Paul Mariani's biography, *William Carlos Williams: A New World Naked* (New York: McGraw-Hill, 1982). For persuasive dissenting opinions about Williams's late poetry, see James E. B. Breslin, *From Modern to Contemporary: American Poetry, 1945–1965* (Chicago: University of Chicago Press, 1983); and Marjorie Perloff, *The Poetics of Indeterminacy: Rimbaud to Cage* (Princeton: Princeton University Press, 1981).

   Critics have begun more recently to rethink the presuppositions informing Williams's academic reception. The motives are various: to trace American avant-garde antecedents to Language poetry (Charles Bernstein, "The Academy in Peril," in *Content's Meaning* [Los Angeles: Sun and Moon, 1986]; Ron Silliman, "Canons and Institutions: New Hope for the Disappeared," in *The Politics of Poetic Form*, ed. Charles Bernstein [New York: Roof, 1990]); to interrogate the critical pretexts for constructions of modernism (Cary Nelson, *Repression and Recovery: Modern American Poetry and the Politics of Cultural Memory, 1910–1945* [Madison, University of Wisconsin Press, 1989]; Bruce Robbins, "Modernism and Professionalism: The Case of William Carlos Williams," *Swiss Papers in English Language and Literature* 2 [1985]: 191–205); or to reconsider the diversity of Williams's writing (Schmidt, *William Carlos Williams, The Arts, and Literary Tradition*).

   6. Writing on Williams and younger poets in her bibliographic essay for *Sixteen Modern American Authors*, Linda Wagner-Martin concludes that "whatever approach the critic takes, it will be partial, limiting, and ultimately frustrating. The quantity of materials is endless; the quality, surprisingly good; and the joy and love of the tributes from poets and critics alike collected in the Terrell *William Carlos Williams: Man and Poet* almost overwhelms the reader." "William Carlos Williams," in *Sixteen Modern American Authors*, vol. 2: *A Survey of Research and Criticism*, ed. Jackson R. Bryer (Durham, N.C.: Duke University Press, 1990), 711. Wagner-Martin's critical overview of Williams scholarship is the best concise account of Williams's academic reception through the 1980s; it builds on the earlier work of Paul Mariani, *William Carlos Williams: The Poet and His Critics* (Chicago: American Library Association, 1975) and Carroll F. Terrell, ed., *William Carlos Williams: Man and Poet* (Orono, Maine: National Poetry Foundation, 1983).

   James E. B. Breslin's writings on Williams's postwar reputation represent the most concerted attempt to delineate Williams's influence on younger poets. See "Introduction: The Presence of Williams in Contemporary Poetry," in *Something to Say: William Carlos Williams on Younger Poets*, ed. James E. B. Breslin (New York: New Directions, 1985), 5–37; and Breslin, *From Modern to Contemporary*. In both books Breslin describes the problematic of belatedness common to postromantic poets, but one intensified by the postmodernist paradox of an avant-garde tradition. He emphasizes Williams's psychological need for affirmation after decades of relative neglect, as well as his desire to guarantee the continuance of his poetics for future generations of writers. Breslin explicitly rejects Harold Bloom's model of literary influence, arguing that influence is not "strictly literary," but his psychological approach similarly tends to reduce the politics of literary history to a struggle for canonization.

7. Nelson, *Repression and Recovery*, 52–53.

8. Ron Silliman, who frequently cites Williams's importance for his own poetic practice, argues more radically that "the mechanisms of public canonization are pathological and its proponents are malignant." "Canons and Institutions," 152. Citing the more recent example of the New American Poetry, Silliman agrees with Nelson that canon formation inevitably results in the "disappearance" of worthwhile poets, as well as the misreading of poets whose poetics do not conform to dominant critical modes of reading. He cogently argues that to contest canons without contesting the institutional structures that canons support merely reinforces their legitimacy. Silliman's distinction between canonization and literary value is especially important for differentiating between literary history and canon formation. Whereas canonization "in generalizing (and, typically, dehistoricizing) aesthetic principles ... subjects the reader to them and obliterates social difference," value is defined by the specificity of the reader: "valuable for whom? to what end?" (153). Like Nelson, Silliman analyzes the institutional structures that enable the production and reception of literary texts. But his argument ultimately relies on a definition of the "academic" reader that replicates the problematic generalizations made about academic poetry by the New American Poets and their proponents.

9. John Rodden, *The Politics of Literary Reputation: The Making and Claiming of "St. George" Orwell* (New York: Oxford University Press, 1989), 63–64.

10. Ibid., 65.

11. In noting that Williams's "rediscovery coincides roughly with declarations of the demise of modernism ... and the birth of post-modernism," Bruce Robbins's brief analysis of the politics of professionalism in Williams's reception cogently articulates the significance of this paradigm shift for his literary reputation. "Modernism and Professionalism," 193.

12. Andreas Huyssen, *After the Great Divide: Modernism, Mass Culture, Postmodernism* (Bloomington: University of Indiana Press, 1986), 192–93.

13. Fredric Jameson, *Postmodernism, or, The Cultural Logic of Late Capitalism* (Durham, N.C.: Duke University Press, 1991), 313–14.

14. The literature on postmodernism has become vast and multifarious. Much of the debate has been concerned with defining the "beginnings" of postmodernism, or postmodernity, as a historical period. Although usually posed as an interdisciplinary problem, arguments for postmodernism's "beginning" usually rely on discipline-specific evidence. This has contributed to the heterogenous interpretations of the politics of postmodernism, especially the politics affiliated with the "new social struggles" of the 1960s and after. I use *postmodernism* as a period term, following Jameson's rigorous formulation of postmodernism in *Postmodernism, or, The Cultural Logic of Late Capitalism*. He argues that the economic preconditions for postmodernism or late capitalism arose in the 1950s, with the cultural manifestations of what we now think of as postmodernism occurring with the psychological and sociological transformations of the 1960s (see Jameson's introduction, especially xviii–xxii). *Postmodernism* is nevertheless most descriptive of writing that evinces the ontological and epistemological effects of postmodernity's historical difference from modernity. I am indebted especially to theories of postmodernism like Huyssen's that analyze the sociopolitical differences between postmodern avant-gardist forms and those of the historical avant-garde. For a brief but interesting correlative to Huyssen's argument on the transformation of the avant-garde in the United States during the 1940s and 1950s, see John Ashbery, "The Invisible Avant-Garde," in *Avant-Garde Art*, ed. Thomas B. Hess and

John Ashbery (New York: Collier, 1967), 124–33. For a thorough socioeconomic analysis of postmodernity, see David Harvey, *The Condition of Postmodernity* (Oxford: Basil Blackwell, 1989). For useful, concise overviews of influential debates on the politics of postmodernism, see the editors' introductions to the following collections of essays: Jonathan Arac, ed., *Postmodernism and Politics* (Minneapolis: University of Minnesota Press, 1986); Hal Foster, ed., *The Anti-Aesthetic: Essays on Postmodern Culture* (Port Townsend, Wash.: Bay Press, 1983); and Andrew Ross, ed., *Universal Abandon? The Politics of Postmodernism* (Minneapolis: University of Minnesota Press, 1988). Hans Bertens's introduction to *Approaching Postmodernism*, ed. Douwe Fokkema and Hans Bertens (Amsterdam: John Benjamins, 1986) provides a comprehensive overview of the term *postmodern*. Finally, for a lucid argument on the politics of postmodernism that draws its evidence primarily from "historiographic metafiction," see Linda Hutcheon, *The Politics of Postmodernism* (New York: Routledge, 1989).

15. M. M. Bakhtin, "Discourse in the Novel," in *The Dialogic Imagination: Four Essays*, ed. Michael Holquist, trans. Caryl Emerson and Michael Holquist (Austin: University of Texas Press, 1981), 361.

16. Richard Terdiman, *Discourse/Counter-Discourse: The Theory and Practice of Symbolic Resistance in Nineteenth-Century France* (Ithaca: Cornell University Press, 1985).

17. Peter Bürger, *Theory of the Avant-Garde*, trans. Michael Shaw (Minneapolis: University of Minnesota Press, 1984), 20–27, 47–54.

18. Walter Benjamin, "The Author as Producer," in *Reflections: Essays, Aphorisms, Autobiographical Writings*, trans. Edmund Jephcott (New York: Harcourt Brace Jovanovich, 1978), 233.

19. William Carlos Williams, "Marianne Moore," in *Imaginations*, ed. Webster Schott (New York: New Directions, 1970), 311.

20. Ibid., 312.

21. Ibid., 314.

22. William Carlos Williams, "Comment," in *Selected Essays of William Carlos Williams*, ed. John C. Thirlwall (New York: Random House, 1954), 28.

23. Charles Tomlinson, introduction to *William Carlos Williams: Selected Poems*, ed. Charles Tomlinson (New York: New Directions, 1985), viii.

24. The radical claims made by the New American Poets for open-form poetics have been criticized of late by critics of various ideological dispositions. In a perceptive analysis of postwar American poetry and ideology, Walter Kaladjian argues that the social text is as absent from the New American Poetry as it is in the "academic poetry" they critique. With few exceptions (most notably, Olson), the New American Poets accept New Critical assumptions about the lyric self and aesthetic autonomy, he argues. See Walter Kaladjian, *Languages of Liberation: The Social Text in Contemporary American Poetry* (New York: Columbia University Press, 1989), 3–32. For a similarly incisive Marxian argument that contrasts the Language poets with the New American Poets, see Andrew Ross, "The New Sentence and the Commodity Form: Recent American Writing," in *Marxism and the Interpretation of Culture*, ed. Cary Nelson and Lawrence Grossberg (Urbana: University of Illinois Press, 1988), 361–80. The collection of essays edited by Robert Frank and Henry Sayre addresses the conventional homology of free-verse poetics and radical politics. See *The Line in Postmodern Poetry* (Urbana: University of Illinois Press, 1988), especially the introduction, where the editors argue that open forms can nonetheless be conceptually closed. Paul Breslin is much less sym-

pathetic to the political impulse of the New American Poetry in his otherwise useful intellectual history of postwar "radical poetics and radical politics." See *The Psycho-Political Muse: American Poetry Since the Fifties* (Chicago: University of Chicago Press, 1987), esp. 1–21. Finally, for a convincing critique of avant-gardist definitions of postmodernism that are based exclusively on the notion of technical progress, see Mutlu Konuk Blasing, "Rethinking Models of Literary Change: The Case of James Merrill," *American Literary History* 2 (1990): 299–317.

25. Mariani, *William Carlos Williams*, 116.

26. On the sexual politics of Williams's appropriation of women's writing, see Sandra M. Gilbert, "Purloined Letters: William Carlos Williams and 'Cress,'" *William Carlos Williams Review* 10.2 (1985): 5–15; and Theodora R. Graham, "Williams, Flossie, and the Others: The Aesthetics of Sexuality," *Contemporary Literature* 28 (1987): 163–86.

27. Breslin, "Introduction: The Presence of Williams in Contemporary Poetry," 7.

28. Ron Silliman, "Language, Realism, Poetry," introduction to *In the American Tree*, ed. Ron Silliman (Orono, Maine: National Poetry Foundation, 1986), xv.

29. T. S. Eliot, "Milton II," in *Selected Prose of T. S. Eliot*, ed. Frank Kermode (New York: Harcourt Brace Jovanovich and Farrar, Straus & Giroux, 1975), 273.

30. Denise Levertov, "William Carlos Williams, 1883–1963," *Nation*, 16 March 1963, reprinted in *The Poet in the World* (New York: New Directions, 1973), 254.

31. LeRoi Jones, "An Interview on *Yugen*," interview by David Ossman, in *The Little Magazine in America: A Modern Documentary History*, ed. Elliott Anderson and Mary Kinzie (Yonkers, N.Y.: Pushcart, 1978), 322.

32. Allen Ginsberg and Robert Duncan, "Early Poetic Community," in *Allen Verbatim: Lectures on Poetry, Politics, Consciousness*, ed. Gordon Ball (New York: McGraw-Hill, 1974), 144.

33. Robert Creeley, "I'm given to write poems," in *A Quick Graph: Collected Notes and Essays*, ed. Donald Allen (San Francisco: Four Seasons, 1970), 65.

34. Gilbert Sorrentino, "*Neon, Kulchur*, etc.," in Anderson and Kinzie, *Little Magazine in America*, 301–2.

35. Ginsberg and Duncan, "Early Poetic Community," 135.

36. Randall Jarrell, "The Situation of a Poet," in *Poetry and the Age* (New York: Knopf, 1953), 244.

37. Thom Gunn's assessment of Williams's "peculiarly healthful influence" is representative of critics who noted Williams's influence while questioning his intellect: "To learn from him, even to imitate him, is not to be dominated by his thought or mannerisms as it often is when we try to learn from Stevens: for Williams has few mannerisms, and his power over rhythm and image is not matched by a power over ideas." "Things, Voices, Minds," review of *The Jacob's Ladder*, by Denise Levertov; *For Love*, by Robert Creeley; *Drowning with Others*, by Robert Watson; *Medusa in Gramercy Park*, by Robert Conquest; *Between Mars and Venus*, by John Hollander; *New and Selected Poems*, by Donald Davie, *Yale Review* 52 (1962): 129.

38. John Guillory, "Canonical and Non-Canonical: A Critique of the Current Debate," *ELH* 54 (1987): 485.

39. Ibid., 516.

40. Williams, introduction to *The Wedge*, in *The Collected Poems of William Carlos Williams*, vol. 2, *1938–1962*, ed. Christopher MacGowan (New York: New Directions, 1988), 55. Williams reprinted this prose introduction in both his *Selected Essays* and *Collected Later Poems*.

Chapter 2. "A Plot of Ground"

Quotations from frequently cited works by Williams hereafter will be cited in the text with the abbreviations listed below:

A: *The Autobiography of William Carlos Williams* (1951; reprint, New York: New Directions, 1967).

CP 1: *The Collected Poems* of William Carlos Williams, vol. 1, *1909–1939*, ed. A. Walton Litz and Christopher MacGowan (New York: New Directions, 1986).

CP 2: *The Collected Poems of William Carlos Williams*, vol. 2, *1938–1962*, ed. Christopher MacGowan (New York: New Directions, 1988).

EK: *The Embodiment of Knowledge*, ed. Ron Loewinsohn (New York: New Directions, 1974).

I: *Imaginations*, containing *Kora in Hell*, 1920; *Spring and All*, 1923; *The Great American Novel*, 1923; *The Descent of Winter*, 1928; *A Novelette and Other Prose*, 1932; ed. Webster Schott (New York: New Directions, 1970).

AG: *In the American Grain* (1925; reprint, New York: New Directions, 1956).

SE: *Selected Essays of William Carlos Williams* (New York: Random House, 1954).

1.   Ezra Pound, "Dr Williams' Position" (1928), reprinted in *Literary Essays of Ezra Pound*, ed. T. S. Eliot (1935; reprint, New York: New Directions, 1968), 390.

2.   Ibid., 392.

3.   Paul Rosenfeld, *Port of New York* (1924; reprint, Urbana: University of Illinois Press: 1966), 109.

4.   Marcus Klein, *Foreigners: The Making of American Literature, 1900–1940* (Chicago: University of Chicago Press, 1981), x.

5.   For overviews of the politics of constructing an Americanist canon in the 1920s, see Russell Reising, *The Unusable Past: Theory and the Study of American Literature* (New York: Methuen, 1986), 13–48; and Paul Lauter, "Race and Gender in the Shaping of the American Literary Canon: A Case Study from the Twenties," *Feminist Studies* 9 (1983): 435–63.

6.   Edward W. Said, *The World, the Text, and the Critic* (Cambridge: Harvard University Press, 1983), 17-24.

7.   Tashjian, *William Carlos Williams and the American Scene*, 101–5.

8.   Ibid., 103.

9.   For Williams's account of the questions surrounding his authorial signature, see Williams, *Autobiography*, 108; and Williams, *I Wanted to Write a Poem: The Autobiography of the Works of a Poet*, reported and edited by Edith Heal (New York: New Directions, 1958), 9. For a compelling analysis of how Williams repressed his mother's Latin American background in creating the myth of himself as an "American" poet, see Julio Marzan, "Mrs. Williams' William Carlos," in *Reinventing the Americas: Comparative Studies of Literature of the United States and Spanish America*, ed. Bell Gale Chevigny and Gari Laguardia (Cambridge: Cambridge University Press, 1986), 106–21.

10. Williams to Marianne Moore, 21 February 1917, in *The Selected Letters of William Carlos Williams*, ed. John C. Thirlwall (New York: McDowell, Oblensky, 1957), 40.

11. Williams, "America, Whitman, and the Art of Poetry" (1917), *William Carlos Williams Review* 13.1 (1987): 2.

12. Ibid., 2–3.

13. On Williams's "local" appropriation of Whitman, see Stephen Tapscott, *American Beauty: William Carlos Williams and the Modernist Whitman* (New York: Columbia University Press, 1984), esp. 21–23, where Williams's "modernist Whitman" is contrasted with Pound's.

14. This reading would assume that the initial descriptive mode of "January Morning" is more naturalistic than the later mode. The poem begins in New Jersey, and then refers to "blue car rails" before reaching the New York ferry. However, the poem purportedly recollects a ferry trip Williams took from Manhattan to New Jersey after staying up all night on duty in a New York hospital. For conflicting interpretations of the poem's narrative plot, see Schmidt, *William Carlos Williams, The Arts, and Literary Tradition*, 64-67; and MacGowan, *William Carlos Williams' Early Poetry*, 29–31.

15. On the "ghost of the Half Moon," see MacGowan, *William Carlos Williams' Early Poetry*, 30.

16. Jonathan Culler, "Apostrophe," in *The Pursuit of Signs: Semiotics, Literature, Deconstruction* (Ithaca: Cornell University Press, 1981), 146.

17. In John C. Thirlwall's annotated copy of *The Collected Earlier Poems*, in which Thirlwall recorded Williams's comments in the late 1950s on individual poems, the note "mother" is recorded beside "old woman." See *CP 1*, 489.

The most thorough analysis of the literary and biographical significance of Williams's relationship with his mother is Kerry Driscoll, *William Carlos Williams and the Maternal Muse* (Ann Arbor, Mich.: UMI Research Press, 1987). Driscoll concentrates primarily on Williams's biography of his mother, *Yes, Mrs Williams*.

18. See, for example, "The Last Words of My Grandmother" (1924), in *CP 1*, 253; and the revision of this poem, "The Last Words of My English Grandmother" (1939), in *CP 1*, 464.

19. This line of literary descent is extended even further in Williams's *Autobiography*: "Grandma remembered more than she would tell of her girlhood in London in the home of the Godwins whose ward she was—the William Godwins, perhaps, who knows?" (4).

20. The coincidence of the identical names has generated some confusion in Dickinson studies. For example, the photograph in the frontispiece of Richard Sewall's *Life of Emily Dickinson*, vol. 2, is actually a photograph of Williams's grandmother. See Hiroko Uno, "Two Emily Dickinsons," *William Carlos Williams Review* 5 (1979): 220–22.

21. J. Hillis Miller, "Presidential Address 1986. The Triumph of Theory, the Resistance to Reading, and the Question of the Material Base," *PMLA* 102 (1987): 282.

22. For an interesting analysis of this issue that compares *In the American Grain* to F. O. Matthiessen's *American Renaissance*, R. W. B. Lewis's *American Adam*, Leo Marx's *Machine in the Garden*, and Richard Poirier's *World Elsewhere*, see James L. Machor, "Tradition, Holism, and the Dilemmas of American Literary Studies," *Texas Studies in Literature and Language* 22 (1980): 99–121.

23. James F. Knapp, "Not Wholeness but Multiplicity: The Primitivism of William Carlos Williams," *Mosaic* 20 (1987): 74.

24. David Bennett, "Defining the 'American' Difference: Cultural Nationalism and the Modernist Poetics of William Carlos Williams," *Southern Review* 20 (1987): 271–80.

25. Ibid., 273.

26. For an excellent comparison of Williams's and Eliot's textual strategies for confronting a common anxiety about the American estrangement from the grounding function of tradition, see Stephen Fredman, "Williams, Eliot, and American Tradition," *Twentieth Century Literature* 35 (1989): 235–53.

27. Vera M. Kutzinski, *Against the American Grain: Myth and History in William Carlos Williams, Jay Wright and Nicholas Guillen* (Baltimore: Johns Hopkins University Press, 1987), 3–46.

28. Bryce Conrad, "Engendering History: The Sexual Structure of William Carlos Williams' *In the American Grain," Twentieth Century Literature* 35 (1989): 260.

29. Miller, "Presidential Address 1986," 287.

30. Williams, however, is guilty of "doctoring" parts of Mather's text that compromise his argument. On Williams's distortion (by excision) of Mather's text, see Breslin, *William Carlos Williams,* 107.

31. Williams's unease about his meeting with Larbaud is shown by his later repression of any memory of this conversation. He makes no reference to Larbaud in his *Autobiography* and actually told his first critical biographer, Vivienne Koch, that he had never met him. However, a diary entry and two letters to Marianne Moore describe their conversation. See Mariani, *William Carlos Williams,* 287; and Williams, *Selected Letters,* 59–60, 63.

CHAPTER 3. "TO WITNESS THE WORDS BEING BORN"

1. George Monteiro examines this conflict between learned professionalism and affective impulses in his study of Williams's doctor stories. See "The Doctor's Black Bag: William Carlos Williams' Passaic River Stories," *Modern Language Studies* 13 (1983): 77–85. See also Breslin, *William Carlos Williams,* 125–67; Robert Coles, *William Carlos Williams: The Knack of Survival in America* (New Brunswick, N.J.: Rutgers University Press, 1975); and Marjorie Perloff, "The Man Who Loved Women: The Medical Fictions of William Carlos Williams," *Georgia Review* 34 (1980): 840–53.

2. Recollecting his early imagist poetry, Williams wrote that "I'm not the type of poet who looks only at the same thing. I want to use the words we speak and to describe the things we see, as far as it can be done. I abandoned the rare world of H.D. and Ezra Pound. Poetry should be brought into the world where we live and not be so recondite, so removed from the people." Quoted by John C. Thirlwall, "William Carlos Williams' 'Paterson,'" *New Directions 17* (New York: New Directions, 1961), 253.

3. The "townspeople poems" have received considerable attention in biographical studies of Williams, however. For a fine reading of these poems in their local political contexts, see David Frail, *The Early Politics and Poetics of William Carlos Williams* (Ann Arbor, Mich.: UMI Research Press, 1987), 109–22.

4. Schmidt, *William Carlos Williams, the Arts, and Literary Tradition,* 10–47.

5. Breslin, *William Carlos Williams,* 52–53.

6. On Williams's affiliations with dadaism, see Dickran Tashjian, *Skyscraper Primitives: Dada and the American Avant-Garde, 1910–1925* (Middletown, Conn.: Wesleyan University Press, 1975). On the impact of cubism on Williams's poetics, see Perloff, *Poetics of Indeterminacy,* 109–54. For detailed studies of the relation of Williams's early poetry—including *Spring and All*—to the visual arts, see Dijkstra, *Hieroglyphics of a New Speech;* MacGowan, *William Carlos Williams' Early Poetry;* Marling, *William Carlos*

Williams and the Painters; Sayre, *The Visual Text of William Carlos Williams;* Schmidt, *William Carlos Williams, the Arts, and Literary Tradition;* and Tashjian, *William Carlos Williams and the American Scene.*

7. Jonathan Monroe, *A Poverty of Objects: The Prose Poem and the Politics of Genre* (Ithaca: Cornell University Press, 1987), 18.

8. Perloff, *Poetics of Indeterminacy,* 137.

9. Although the poems were untitled in the original version of *Spring and All,* I will refer to them by their later titles when discussing them individually.

10. Hugh Kenner, *A Homemade World: The American Modernist Writers* (New York: Morrow, 1975), 86.

11. There are references in poems throughout *Spring and All* to the anonymous, the unarticulated. See, for example, "Flight to the City" (*CP 1,* 186–87); "The Right of Way" (*CP 1,* 205–6); and "The Avenue of Poplars" (*CP 1,* 228–29).

12. Frail, *Early Politics and Poetics of William Carlos Williams,* 80–81.

13. As J. Hillis Miller argues, *Spring and All*'s theory of imagination is ultimately Aristotelian. See "Williams' 'Spring and All' and the Progress of Poetry," *Daedalus* 94 (1970): 415–29.

14. Louis Zukofsky, "American Poetry, 1920–1930" (1930), reprinted in *Prepositions: The Collected Critical Essays of Louis Zukofsky,* expanded ed. (Berkeley: University of California Press, 1981), 150.

15. James Clifford, "Introduction: The Pure Products Go Crazy," in *The Predicament of Culture: Twentieth-Century Ethnography, Literature, and Art* (Cambridge: Harvard University Press, 1988), 3.

16. Ibid., 6.

17. Ibid., 7.

18. Frail, *Early Politics and Poetics of William Carlos Williams,* 185–88.

CHAPTER 4. "PURE PRODUCTS"

1. Laughlin letter to Williams, 11 October 1960, in William Carlos Williams and James Laughlin, *Selected Letters,* ed. Hugh Witemeyer (New York: Norton, 1989), 238.

2. Ibid., 239.

3. See W. Jackson Bate, *The Burden of the Past and the English Poet* (New York: Norton, 1970); and Harold Bloom, *The Anxiety of Influence: A Theory of Poetry* (New York: Oxford University Press, 1975).

4. Sandra M. Gilbert and Susan Gubar, *No Man's Land: The Place of the Woman Writer in the Twentieth Century,* vol. 1: *The War of the Words* (New Haven: Yale University Press, 1988), 168.

5. Ibid., 184.

6. On the editing and publication of *The Wedge,* see Neil Baldwin, "Zukofsky, Williams, and *The Wedge:* Toward a Dynamic Convergence," in *Louis Zukofsky: Man and Poet,* ed. Carroll F. Terrell (Orono, Maine: National Poetry Foundation, 1979), 129–42; and Mariani, *William Carlos Williams,* 480–83.

7. Denise Levertov, *Collected Earlier Poems, 1940–1960* (New York: New Directions, 1979), 3. Quotations of Levertov's books of poetry will hereafter be cited in the text with the following abbreviations:

CEP: *Collected Earlier Poems, 1940–1960* (New York: New Directions, 1979).

P: *Poems, 1960–1967* (New York: New Directions, 1983).

8. Levertov, "Some Duncan Letters—A Memoir and a Critical Tribute" (1979), reprinted in *Light Up the Cave* (New York: New Directions, 1981), 201.

9. As Levertov explains in her "Author's Note" to *Collected Earlier Poems*, the division of the poems into two books was somewhat "arbitrary," rather than the result of any change in her development as a poet (viii–ix). She had promised to publish collections for both City Lights Books and Jargon Books. *Here and Now* is comprised of the poems selected by Lawrence Ferlinghetti, while *Overland to the Islands* includes poems rejected by Ferlinghetti as well as several later poems.

10. Although Levertov lived primarily in New York during the 1950s, she also lived in Mexico for several years.

11. Breslin, *From Modern to Contemporary*, 145. What Breslin perceives as lack of ambition can also be seen as evidence of the ambition of a poet who, after all, was one of the few to appear in both *The New American Poetry* and *New Poets of England and America* (1962 ed.). Ron Silliman, for example, has suggested that her use of familiar modernist forms and styles have made her more likely to receive widespread acclaim. See Silliman, "Canons and Institutions," 154–56. For a detailed overview of Levertov's critical reception, see Linda Sakeilliou-Schultz, *Denise Levertov: An Annotated Primary and Secondary Bibliography* (New York: Garland, 1988).

12. See especially Breslin, *From Modern to Contemporary*; Suzanne Juhasz, *Naked and Fiery Forms: Modern American Poetry by Women, A New Tradition* (New York: Farrar, Straus & Giroux, 1976), 57–84; Ralph J. Mills, "Denise Levertov: Poetry of the Immediate," reprinted in *Denise Levertov: In Her Own Province*, ed. Linda Welshimer Wagner (New York: New Directions, 1979), 103–18; Diana Surman, "Inside and Outside in the Poetry of Denise Levertov," *Critical Quarterly* 22 (1980): 57–70; and Linda Welshimer Wagner, *Denise Levertov* (Boston: Twayne, 1967).

13. Levertov, "Poems by Women," in Wagner, *Denise Levertov: In Her Own Province*, 99.

14. Ibid., 100.

15. Sandra M. Gilbert, "Revolutionary Love: Denise Levertov and the Poetics of Politics," *Parnassus: Poetry in Review* 12 (1985): 336. Gilbert borrows the appellation "poet of revolutionary love" from Levertov's essay, "Poetry and Revolution: Neruda Is Dead—Neruda Lives" (1973), reprinted in *Light Up the Cave*, 133. She is more skeptical, however, about the "revolutionary" stance of Levertov's more explicitly political poems; she argues that Levertov is not primarily an artist of irony or disillusionment.

16. See especially Juhasz, *Naked and Fiery Forms*, 57–84; Alicia Ostriker, "In Mind: The Divided Self in Women's Poetry," in *Poetics: Essays on the Art of Poetry*, ed. Paul Mariani and George Murphy (Ocean Bluff, Mass.: Tendril, 1984), 111–38; and Deborah Pope, *A Separate Vision: Isolation in Contemporary Women's Poetry* (Baton Rouge: Louisiana State University Press, 1984), 84–115.

17. Rachel Blau DuPlessis, "The Critique of Consciousness and Myth in Levertov, Rich and Rukeyser," in *Shakespeare's Sisters: Feminist Essays on Women Poets*, ed. Sandra M. Gilbert and Susan Gubar (Bloomington: Indiana University Press, 1979), 279–300. DuPlessis's argument is especially relevant for Levertov's Vietnam War protest poetry, which has divided her critics. She argues that the poetry collected in *To Stay Alive* self-consciously records an impasse about inwardness as a path to social transformation (290–91). A number of Levertov's readers have been more critical of this poetry, agreeing with Bonnie Costello's assessment that the relation between Levertov's public and private selves has always seemed "a bit strained, a bit superficial"; her symmetries thus appear "posed and inauthentic." Bonnie Costello, "Flooded with Otherness," review of

Freeing the Dust, Life in the Forest, and *Collected Earlier Poems, 1940–1960,* by Denise Levertov, *Parnassus: Poetry in Review* 8.1 (1979): 198. Several critics have argued that the weakness of this public stance results from the limitations of her poetic stance. Cary Nelson argues that Levertov's Vietnam War protest poetry exemplifies the American poetic myth that personal articulation can cleanse language, that the poet's speech can be sacrificed for the revitalization of the American language. See Cary Nelson, *Our Last First Poets: Vision and History in Contemporary Poetry* (Urbana: University of Illinois Press, 1981), 16–21. According to Nelson, Levertov's poetry signifies the "end of a poetic of open optimism" (21); her antiwar poems are "passionate quests . . . generated by internal needs, . . . motivated by self-interest; at worst, they are ironically a kind of poetic colonialism, pathetic evidence that our history shapes and uses our poetry whatever our intentions" (17). Charles Altieri agrees with Nelson but emphasizes that a poetics of immanence such as hers "tends toward passivity; using strategies of perception to explore evil makes the self helpless in relation to social forces." Charles Altieri, *Enlarging the Temple: New Directions in American Poetry during the 1960s* (Lewisburg, Pa.: Bucknell University Press, 1979), 237. For a strident amplification of Altieri's argument, see Paul Breslin, *The Psycho-Political Muse,* 203–5. For a cogent critique of Altieri's analysis of Levertov's poetry, see Richard Jackson, *The Dismantling of Time in Contemporary Poetry* (Tuscaloosa: University of Alabama Press, 1988), 187–238. Jackson argues that presence is always qualified in her poetry; because there is a characteristic movement in her poetry toward contexts or toward other times that invades the moment of pure presence, her political poems are more consistent with the general patterns of her work than Altieri claims.

 These indictments of Levertov's Vietnam War protest poetry cite these poems as exemplary failures of an inherently private stance to speak publicly. Significantly, the harshest condemnations of this poetry tend to ignore feminist studies of the "split self" in her earlier poetry. Critics who praise her antiwar poetry argue that her stance unites political commitment with woman's experience. See, for example, Kerry Driscoll, "A Sense of Unremitting Emergency: Politics in the Early Work of Denise Levertov," *Centennial Review* 30 (1986): 292–303; Juhasz, *Naked and Fiery Forms,* 57–84; and Lorrie Smith, "Songs of Experience: Denise Levertov's Political Poetry," *Contemporary Literature* 27 (1986): 213–32.

 18. Denise Levertov, "The Sense of Pilgrimage" (1968), reprinted in *The Poet in the World* (New York: New Directions, 1973), 80.

 19. Denise Levertov, "Great Possessions," in *Poet in the World,* 90.

 20. Ibid., 93–94.

 21. Ibid., 97–98.

 22. Ibid., 100.

 23. Denise Levertov, "On the Function of the Line" (1979), reprinted in *Light Up the Cave,* 61.

 24. Ibid., 61–62.

 25. This letter is quoted in Levertov, "Rilke as Mentor," *Light up the Cave,* 288.

 26. Letter quoted in Levertov, "Rilke as Mentor," in *Light up the Cave,* 287.

 27. Levertov, "Rilke as Mentor," 285.

 28. For example, "Something" begins with a portrayal of "the tall women on Madison / sniffing, peering at windows" (*CEP,* 61), a portrayal that is simultaneously grotesque and pitiful. The women hunting for hats are reduced to "sniffing, peering" animal figures, a fitting introductory image for the indictment of that "monster," capitalist greed, that follows. "Poem from Manhattan" similarly represents a city motivated by

the greed for consumer goods, which results in the unsettling contrasts of poverty and wealth: "the derelict & the diamond-sharp" (*CEP*, 52).

29. Denise Levertov, "The Ideas in the Things," in *William Carlos Williams: Man and Poet*, ed. Carroll F. Terrell (Orono, Maine: National Poetry Foundation, 1983), 142.

30. Denise Levertov, "On the Edge of Darkness: What Is Political Poetry?" in *Light Up the Cave*, 121.

31. Ibid., 126.

32. Ibid., 128.

Chapter 5. "Going to sleep with quandariness"

Quotations from O'Hara's *Collected Poems* will hereafter be cited in the text parenthetically with the abbreviation *CP*.

1. O'Hara substituted his "Statement for *New American Poetry*" for "Personism." He eventually published "Personism" in *Yugen* 7 (1961).

2. Helen Vendler, *Part of Nature, Part of Us: Modern American Poets* (Cambridge: Harvard University Press, 1980), 183.

3. Frank O'Hara, *Lunch Poems* (San Francisco: City Lights, 1964), back cover.

4. For a compelling critique of how the critical reception of O'Hara has repressed the political implications of gay language practices in his poetry, see Bruce Boone, "Gay Language as Political Practice: The Poetry of Frank O'Hara," *Social Text* 1 (1979): 59–72.

5. The most detailed account of O'Hara's appropriation of Williams's technique remains Marjorie Perloff, *Frank O'Hara: Poet Among the Painters* (Austin: University of Texas Press), esp. 38, 44–48, 54–56. See also Mutlu Konuk Blasing, *The Art of Life: Studies in American Autobiographical Literature* (Austin: University of Texas Press, 1977), 113–56, esp. 139; Peter Baker, *Modern Poetic Practice: Structure and Genesis* (New York: Peter Lang, 1986), 177–206; Charles Molesworth, *The Fierce Embrace: A Study of Contemporary American Poetry* (Columbia: University of Missouri Press, 1979), 20; and Breslin, *From Modern to Contemporary*, 218.

6. On O'Hara's reading of Williams, see Perloff, *Frank O'Hara*, 45.

7. See the first chapter of Perloff, *Poetics of Indeterminacy*, 3–44, on the significance of "indeterminacy" in modern and postmodern poetry, and Altieri, *Enlarging the Temple*, on the poetics of "immanence."

8. Fredric Jameson, foreword to *The Postmodern Condition: A Report on Knowledge*, by Jean-François Lyotard, trans. Geoff Bennington and Brian Massumi (Minneapolis: University of Minnesota Press, 1984), xviii.

9. Fredric Jameson, "Postmodernism and Consumer Society," in Foster, *Anti-Aesthetic*, 115.

10. See Huyssen, *After the Great Divide*, and Linda Hutcheon, *The Politics of Postmodernism* (New York: Routledge, 1989).

11. Charles Jencks, *What is Postmodernism?*, rev. ed. (New York: St. Martin's, 1987), 14.

12. Perloff, *Frank O'Hara*, 48–51.

13. Gertrude Stein, "Picasso" (1938), in *Picasso: The Complete Writings*, ed. Edward Burns (Boston: Beacon, 1985), 37.

14. O'Hara, "American Art and Non-American Art" (1959), in *Standing Still and Walking in New York* (Bolinas, Calif.: Grey Fox, 1975), 97.

15. Ibid., 98.

16. O'Hara, interview by Edward Lucie-Smith (1965), in *Standing Still and Walking in New York*, 9.

17. O'Hara, *Jackson Pollock* (New York: Braziller, 1959), 22.

18. Ibid., 21.

19. Mutlu Konuk Blasing, *American Poetry: The Rhetoric of Its Forms* (New Haven: Yale University Press, 1987), 158.

20. O'Hara, *Jackson Pollock*, 16.

21. Ibid.

22. Ibid., 11.

23. Despite the prominence of war imagery in O'Hara's early poetry, this topic has received surprisingly little attention. O'Hara himself was reticent about his war experiences. According to Joe LeSueur, in over nine years of living with him, O'Hara never spoke about "what he did in the war." LeSueur, introduction to *Selected Plays*, by Frank O'Hara (New York: Full Court Press, 1978), x. The fullest account of O'Hara's years in the navy can be found in an essay he wrote while at Harvard, "Lament and Chastisement: A Travelogue of War and Personality." See O'Hara, *Early Writing*, ed. Donald Allen (Bolinas, Calif.: Grey Fox, 1977), 112–31.

24. O'Hara, interview by Edward Lucie-Smith, *Standing Still and Walking in New York*, 21.

25. Roland Barthes, *S/Z*, trans. Richard Miller (New York: Hill and Wang, 1974), 51.

26. Vendler, *Part of Nature, Part of Us*, 183.

27. Molesworth, *Fierce Embrace*, 19.

28. Robert von Hallberg, *American Poetry and American Culture, 1945–1980* (Cambridge: Harvard University Press, 1985), 178.

29. Altieri, *Enlarging the Temple*, 120-22.

30. Harold Rosenberg, *The Anxious Object: Art Today and its Audience* (New York: Horizon Press, 1964), 45-46.

31. Frank O'Hara, "Nature and New Painting," in *Standing Still and Walking in New York*, 42.

32. George Simmel, "The Metropolis and Mental Life," in *The Sociology of Georg Simmel*, trans. and ed. Kurt H. Woolf (Glencoe, Ill.: Free Press, 1950), 422.

33. Ibid., 414.

CHAPTER 6. "WORDS WE HAVE LEARNED NOT TO LOOK AT"

Quotations from Oppen's *Collected Poems* will hereafter be cited within the text parenthetically with the abbreviation *CP*.

1. Oppen questioned whether such an emphasis on opposing literary affiliations obscured other, more pressing, political issues. In a letter to his sister, June Oppen Degnan, shortly after President Kennedy's assassination, he wrote: "I saw LeRoi Jones—who has been feeling very left-rebellious—at the [Lita] Hornick party. . . . The war-games of the Beats and Academics look a little silly—with the vandals outside, I told him. And we agreed." Oppen to June Oppen Degnan, 24 November 1963, in *The Selected*

Letters of George Oppen, ed. Rachel Blau DuPlessis (Durham, N.C.: Duke University Press, 1990), 96.

2. See Ron Silliman, "Third Phase Objectivism," *Paideuma* 10 (Spring 1981): 85–89.

3. Oppen to June Oppen Degnan, 9 February 1959, in *Selected Letters*, 25–26. June Oppen Degnan, Oppen's half-sister, was the publisher of *San Francisco Review*, and copublisher, with New Directions, of *The Materials* (1962) and *This in Which* (1965), Oppen's second and third books.

4. For informative comparisons of Oppen's and Williams's prosodies, see Eleanor Berry, "The Williams-Oppen Connection," *Sagetrieb* 3 (Fall 1984): 99–116; and Marjorie Perloff, "The Shape of the Lines: Oppen and the Metric of Difference," in *George Oppen: Man and Poet*, ed. Burton Hatlen (Orono, Maine: National Poetry Foundation, 1981), 25–29.

5. Perloff, "The Shape of the Lines," 229.

6. Michael André Bernstein cogently explains the significance of this contradictory epistemology for Oppen's poetics in his brief essay, "Reticence and Rhetorics: The Poetry of George Oppen," in Hatlen, *George Oppen: Man and Poet*, 231-37.

7. For contrasting accounts of whether Oppen's poetry of the 1960s resolves this contradiction, see Burton Hatlen, "'Not Altogether Lone in a Lone Universe': George Oppen's *The Materials*," in Hatlen, *George Oppen: Man and Poet*, 325–57; and Marjorie Perloff, "The Shipwreck of the Singular: George Oppen's 'Of Being Numerous,'" in Hatlen, *George Oppen: Man and Poet*, 193–204.

8. William Carlos Williams, "The New Poetical Economy" (1934), reprinted in Hatlen, *George Oppen: Man and Poet*, 268.

9. Louis Zukofsky, "Program: 'Objectivists' 1931," *Poetry* 38 (February 1931): 268.

10. Oppen, interview by L. S. Dembo (1969), reprinted in *The Contemporary Writer: Interviews with Sixteen Novelists and Poets*, ed. L. S. Dembo and Cyrena N. Pondrom (Madison: University of Wisconsin Press, 1972), 173.

11. Oppen to John Taggart, 28 March 1973, in *Selected Letters*, 262.

12. Oppen, "Three Poets," review of *Kaddish and Other Poems, 1958–1960*, by Allen Ginsberg; *Maximus from Dogtown*, by Charles Olson; *The Distances*, by Charles Olson; and *Dark Brown*, by Michael McClure, *Poetry* 100 (August 1962): 331–32.

13. Oppen, interview by L. S. Dembo, 183. Rachel Blau DuPlessis delineates Oppen's critique of Pound's rhetorical stance in "Objectivist Poetics and Political Vision: A Study of Oppen and Pound," in Hatlen, *George Oppen: Man and Poet*, 123–48.

14. Oppen explains the circumstances of this essay's composition in a letter to June Oppen Degnan. He writes that this essay, which Levertov rejected for publication, "very nearly tells her to stop writing for a while—if she must, just now, arrive at edifying conclusions. or comforting conclusions." Oppen to June Oppen Degnan, mid-1962, in *Selected Letters*, 58. Oppen praises and defends Levertov's poetry on several occasions elsewhere, however. See, for example, Oppen to Lita Hornick, Summer 1965, in *Selected Letters*, 115–16; and to Dan Gerber, 27 November 1970, in *Selected Letters*, 218.

15. Oppen, "The Mind's Own Place," *Kulchur* 10 (Summer 1963): 3.

16. Ibid., 4.

17. Oppen to June Oppen Degnan, May 1963, in *Selected Letters*, 85.

18. Oppen, "The Mind's Own Place," 5.

19. Ibid., 6.

20. Robert von Hallberg, "The Politics of Description: William Carlos Williams in the Thirties," *ELH* 45 (1978): 131–51.

21. Oppen, interview by L. S. Dembo, 187.

22. Oppen to Linda Oppen Mourelatos, 2 April 1966, in *Selected Letters*, 132.

23. Oppen to Serge Fauchereau, 25 July 1966, in *Selected Letters*, 142.

24. Mary Oppen, *Meaning a Life: An Autobiography* (Santa Barbara, Calif.: Black Sparrow, 1978), 68.

25. Oppen, "Statement on Poetics," *Sagetrieb* 3 (Winter 1984): 26.

26. Oppen to June Oppen Degnan, late 1963–early 1964(?), in *Selected Letters*, 98–99.

Bibliography

Allen, Donald M. Preface to *The Postmoderns: The New American Poetry Revised*, edited by Donald M. Allen and George F. Butterick. New York: Grove, 1982.

——, ed. *The New American Poetry*. New York: Grove, 1960.

Altieri, Charles. *Enlarging the Temple: New Directions in American Poetry during the 1960s*. Lewisburg, Pa.: Bucknell University Press, 1979.

Antin, David. "Modernism and Postmodernism: Approaching the Present in American Poetry." *Boundary 2* 1 (1972): 98–133.

Arac, Jonathan, ed. *Postmodernism and Politics*. Minneapolis: University of Minnesota Press, 1986.

Ashbery, John. "The Invisible Avant-Garde." In *Avant-Garde Art*, edited by Thomas B. Hess and John Ashbery. New York: Collier, 1967.

Baker, Peter. *Modern Poetic Practice: Structure and Genesis*. New York: Peter Lang, 1986.

Bakhtin, M. M. *The Dialogic Imagination: Four Essays*. Edited by Michael Holquist. Translated by Caryl Emerson and Michael Holquist. Austin: University of Texas Press, 1981.

Baldwin, Neil. "Zukofsky, Williams and *The Wedge*: Toward a Dynamic Convergence." In *Louis Zukofsky: Man and Poet*, edited by Carroll F. Terrell. Orono, Maine: National Poetry Foundation, 1979.

Barthes, Roland. *S/Z*. Translated by Richard Miller. New York: Hill and Wang, 1974.

Bate, W. Jackson. *The Burden of the Past and the English Poet*. New York: Norton, 1970.

Benjamin, Walter. "The Author as Producer." In *Reflections: Essays, Aphorisms, Autobiographical Writings*, translated by Edmund Jephcott. New York: Harcourt Brace Jovanovich, 1978.

Bennett, David. "Defining the 'American' Difference: Cultural Nationalism and the Modernist Poetics of William Carlos Williams." *Southern Review* 20 (1987): 271–80.

Benveniste, Emile. *Problems in General Linguistics*. Translated by Mary Elizabeth Meek. Coral Gables, Fla.: University of Miami Press, 1971.

Bernstein, Charles. "The Academy in Peril: William Carlos Williams Meets the MLA." In *Content's Dream: Essays, 1975–1984*. Los Angeles: Sun and Moon, 1986.

Bernstein, Michael André. "Reticence and Rhetorics: The Poetry of George Oppen." In *George Oppen: Man and Poet*, edited by Burton Hatlen. Orono, Maine: National Poetry Foundation, 1981.

162

Berry, Eleanor. "The Williams-Oppen Connection." *Sagetrieb* 3 (Fall 1984): 99–116.

Blasing, Mutlu Konuk. *American Poetry: The Rhetoric of Its Forms.* New Haven: Yale University Press, 1987.

———. *The Art of Life: Studies in American Autobiographical Literature.* Austin: University of Texas Press, 1977.

———. "Rethinking Models of Literary Change: The Case of James Merrill." *American Literary History* 2 (1990): 299–317.

Bloom, Harold. *The Anxiety of Influence: A Theory of Poetry.* New York: Oxford University Press, 1975.

Bogan, Louise. Review of *The New American Poetry*, edited by Donald M. Allen. *New Yorker*, 8 October 1960, 199–200.

Boone, Bruce. "Gay Language as Political Practice: The Poetry of Frank O'Hara." *Social Text* 1 (1979): 59–72.

Breslin, James E. B. *From Modern to Contemporary: American Poetry, 1945–1965.* Chicago: University of Chicago Press, 1983.

———. "Introduction: The Presence of Williams in Contemporary Poetry." In *Something to Say: William Carlos Williams on Younger Poets*, edited by James E. B. Breslin. New York: New Directions, 1985.

———. *William Carlos Williams: An American Artist.* New York: Oxford University Press, 1970.

Breslin, Paul. *The Psycho-Political Muse: American Poetry Since the Fifties.* Chicago: University of Chicago Press, 1987.

Brooks, Van Wyk. "America's Coming of Age." In *Three Essays on America.* 1934. New York: Dutton, 1970.

Bürger, Peter. *Theory of the Avant-Garde.* Translated by Michael Shaw. Minneapolis: University of Minnesota Press, 1984.

Clifford, James. "Introduction: The Pure Products Go Crazy." In *The Predicament of Culture: Twentieth-Century Ethnography, Literature, and Art.* Cambridge: Harvard University Press, 1988.

Coles, Robert. *William Carlos Williams: The Knack of Survival in America.* New Brunswick, N.J.: Rutgers University Press, 1975.

Conrad, Bryce. "Engendering History: The Sexual Structure of William Carlos Williams' *In the American Grain*." *Twentieth Century Literature* 35 (1989): 254–78.

Costello, Bonnie. "Flooded with Otherness." Review of *Freeing the Dust, Life in the Forest, Collected Earlier Poems: 1940–1960*, by Denise Levertov. *Parnassus: Poetry in Review* 8.1 (1979): 198–212.

Creeley, Robert. "I'm given to write poems." In *A Quick Graph: Collected Notes and Essays*, edited by Donald Allen. San Francisco: Four Seasons, 1970.

Culler, Jonathan. "Apostrophe." In *The Pursuit of Signs: Semiotics, Literature, Deconstruction.* Ithaca: Cornell University Press, 1981.

Dijkstra, Bram. *The Hieroglyphics of a New Speech: Cubism, Stieglitz, and the Early Poetry of William Carlos Williams.* Princeton: Princeton University Press, 1969.

Driscoll, Kerry. "A Sense of Unremitting Emergency: Politics in the Early Work of Denise Levertov." *The Centennial Review* 30 (1986): 292–303.

———. *William Carlos Williams and the Maternal Muse.* Ann Arbor, Mich.: UMI Research Press, 1987.

DuPlessis, Rachel Blau. "The Critique of Consciousness and Myth in Levertov, Rich and Rukeyser." In *Shakespeare's Sisters: Feminist Essays on Women Poets*, edited by Sandra M. Gilbert and Susan Gubar. Bloomington: Indiana University Press, 1979.

———. "Objectivist Poetics and Political Vision: A Study of Oppen and Pound." In *George Oppen: Man and Poet*, edited by Burton Hatlen. Orono, Maine: National Poetry Foundation, 1981.

Eliot, T. S. *Selected Prose of T. S. Eliot*. Edited by Frank Kermode. New York: Harcourt Brace Jovanovich and Farrar, Straus & Giroux, 1975.

Fokkema, Douwe, and Hans Bertens, eds. *Approaching Postmodernism*. Amsterdam: John Benjamins, 1986.

Foster, Hal, ed. *The Anti-Aesthetic: Essays on Postmodern Culture*. Port Townsend, Wash.: Bay Press, 1983.

Frail, David. *The Early Politics and Poetics of William Carlos Williams*. Ann Arbor, Mich.: UMI Research Press, 1987.

Frank, Robert, and Henry Sayre, eds. *The Line in Postmodern Poetry*. Urbana: University of Illinois Press, 1988.

Frank, Waldo. *Our America*. New York: Boni, 1919.

Fredman, Stephen. "Williams, Eliot, and American Tradition." *Twentieth Century Literature* 35 (1989): 235–53.

Gilbert, Sandra M. "Purloined Letters: William Carlos Williams and 'Cress.'" *William Carlos Williams Review* 10.2 (1985): 5–15.

———. "Revolutionary Love: Denise Levertov and the Poetics of Politics." *Parnassus: Poetry in Review* 12 (1985): 335–51.

Gilbert, Sandra M., and Susan Gubar. *No Man's Land: The Place of the Woman Writer in the Twentieth Century*. Vol. 1, *The War of the Words*. New Haven: Yale University Press, 1988.

Ginsberg, Allen, and Robert Duncan. "Early Poetic Community." In *Allen Verbatim: Lectures on Poetry, Politics, Consciousness*, edited by Gordon Ball. New York: McGraw-Hill, 1974.

Golding, Alan C. "A History of American Poetry Anthologies." In *Canons*, edited by Robert von Hallberg. Chicago: University of Chicago Press, 1984.

Graham, Theodora R. "Williams, Flossie, and the Others: The Aesthetics of Sexuality." *Contemporary Literature* 28 (1987): 163–86.

Guillory, John. "Canonical and Non-Canonical: A Critique of the Current Debate." *ELH* 54 (1987): 483–527.

Guimond, James. *The Art of William Carlos Williams: A Discovery and Possession of America*. Urbana: University of Illinois Press, 1968.

Gunn, Thom. "Things, Voices, Minds." Review of *The Jacob's Ladder*, by Denise Levertov; *For Love*, by Robert Creeley; *Drowning with Others*, by Robert Watson; *Medusa in Gramercy Park*, by Robert Conquest; *Between Mars and Venus*, by John Hollander; *New and Selected Poems*, by Donald Davie. *The Yale Review* 52 (1962): 129–38.

Hall, Donald, Robert Pack, and Louis Simpson, eds. *New Poets of England and America*. New York: New American Library, 1957.

Harvey, David. *The Condition of Postmodernity*. Oxford: Basil Blackwell, 1989.

Hatlen, Burton. "'Not Altogether Lone in a Lone Universe': George Oppen's *The*

Materials." In *George Oppen: Man and Poet*, edited by Burton Hatlen. Orono, Maine: National Poetry Foundation, 1981.

Hutcheon, Linda. *The Politics of Postmodernism*. New York: Routledge, 1989.

Huyssen, Andreas. *After the Great Divide: Modernism, Mass Culture, Postmodernism.* Bloomington: Indiana University Press, 1986.

Jackson, Richard. *The Dismantling of Time in Contemporary Poetry*. Tuscaloosa: University of Alabama Press, 1988.

Jameson, Fredric. Foreword to *The Postmodern Condition: A Report on Knowledge*, by Jean-François Lyotard. Translated by Geoff Bennington and Brian Massumi. Minneapolis: University of Minnesota Press, 1984.

———. *Postmodernism, or, the Cultural Logic of Late Capitalism*. Durham, N.C.: Duke University Press, 1991.

———. "Postmodernism and Consumer Society." In *The Anti-Aesthetic: Essays on Postmodern Culture*, edited by Hal Foster. Port Townsend, Wash.: Bay Press, 1983.

Jarrell, Randall. "The Situation of a Poet." In *Poetry and the Age*. New York: Knopf, 1953.

Jencks, Charles. *What Is Postmodernism?* Rev. ed. New York: St. Martin's, 1987.

Jones, LeRoi. "An Interview on *Yugen*." By David Ossman. 1960. Reprinted in *The Little Magazine in America: A Modern Documentary History*, edited by Elliott Anderson and Mary Kinzie. Yonkers, N.Y.: Pushcart, 1978.

Juhasz, Suzanne. *Naked and Fiery Forms: Modern American Poetry by Women, A New Tradition*. New York: Farrar, Straus & Giroux, 1976.

Kaladjian, Walter. *Languages of Liberation: The Social Text in Contemporary American Poetry*. New York: Columbia University Press, 1989.

Kenner, Hugh. *A Homemade World: The American Modernist Writers*. New York: Morrow, 1975.

Klein, Marcus. *Foreigners: The Making of American Literature, 1900–1940*. Chicago: University of Chicago Press, 1981.

Knapp, James F. "Not Wholeness but Multiplicity: The Primitivism of William Carlos Williams." *Mosaic* 20 (1987): 71–81.

Kutzinski, Vera M. *Against the American Grain: Myth and History in William Carlos Williams, Jay Wright and Nicholas Guillen*. Baltimore: Johns Hopkins University Press, 1987.

Lauter, Paul. "Race and Gender in the Shaping of the American Literary Canon: A Case Study from the Twenties." *Feminist Studies* 9 (1983): 435–63.

Lawrence, D. H. *Studies in Classic American Literature*. 1923. New York: Viking, 1964.

LeSueur, Joe. Introduction to *Selected Plays*, by Frank O'Hara. New York: Full Court Press, 1978.

Levertov, Denise. *Collected Earlier Poems, 1940–1960*. New York: New Directions, 1979.

———. "The Ideas in the Things." In *William Carlos Williams: Man and Poet*, edited by Carroll F. Terrell. Orono, Maine: National Poetry Foundation, 1983.

———. *Light up the Cave*. New York: New Directions, 1981.

———. *Poems, 1960–1967*. New York: New Directions, 1983.

———. "Poems by Women." In *Denise Levertov: In Her Own Province*, edited by Linda Welshimer Wagner. New York: New Directions, 1979.

———. *The Poet in the World*. New York: New Directions, 1973.

MacGowan, Christopher. *William Carlos Williams' Early Poetry: The Visual Arts Background*. Ann Arbor, Mich.: UMI Research Press, 1984.

Machor, James L. "Tradition, Holism, and the Dilemmas of American Literary Studies." *Texas Studies in Literature and Language* 22 (1980): 99–121.

Macksey, Richard A. "'A Certainty of Music': Williams' Changes." In *William Carlos Williams: A Collection of Critical Essays*, edited by J. Hillis Miller. Englewood Cliffs, N. J.: Prentice-Hall, 1966.

Mariani, Paul. *William Carlos Williams: A New World Naked*. New York: McGraw-Hill, 1982.

———. *William Carlos Williams: The Poet and His Critics*. Chicago: American Library Association, 1975.

Marling, William. *William Carlos Williams and the Painters, 1909–1923*. Athens: Ohio University Press, 1982.

Marzan, Julio. "Mrs. Williams' William Carlos." In *Reinventing the Americas: Comparative Studies of Literature of the United States and Spanish America*, edited by Bell Gale Chevigny and Gari Laguardia. Cambridge: Cambridge University Press, 1986.

Miller, J. Hillis. *Poets of Reality: Six Twentieth-Century Writers*. Cambridge: Belknap Press of Harvard University Press, 1966.

———. "Presidential Address 1986. The Triumph of Theory, the Resistance to Reading, and the Question of the Material Base." *PMLA* 102 (1987): 281–91.

———. "Williams' *Spring and All* and the Progress of Poetry." *Daedalus* 94 (1970): 415–29.

Mills, Ralph J. "Denise Levertov: Poetry of the Immediate." 1965. Reprinted in *Denise Levertov: In Her Own Province*, edited by Linda Welshimer Wagner. New York: New Directions, 1979.

Molesworth, Charles. *The Fierce Embrace: A Study of Contemporary American Poetry*. Columbia: University of Missouri Press, 1979.

Monroe, Jonathan. *A Poverty of Objects: The Prose Poem and the Politics of Genre*. Ithaca: Cornell University Press, 1987.

Monteiro, George. "The Doctor's Black Bag: William Carlos Williams' Passaic River Stories." *Modern Language Studies* 13 (1983): 77–85.

Moore, Marianne. "Archaically New (A comment accompanying three poems by Elizabeth Bishop, 'The Reprimands,' 'The Map,' and 'Three Valentines')." In *The Complete Prose of Marianne Moore*, edited by Patricia C. Willis. New York: Viking, 1986.

Nelson, Cary. *Our Last First Poets: Vision and History in Contemporary Poetry*. Urbana: University of Illinois Press, 1981.

———. *Repression and Recovery: Modern American Poetry and the Politics of Cultural Memory, 1910–1945*. Madison: University of Wisconsin Press, 1989.

Noble, David W. *The End of American History: Democracy, Capitalism and the Metaphor of Two Worlds in Anglo-American Historical Writing, 1880–1980*. Minneapolis: University of Minnesota Press, 1985.

O'Hara, Frank. *The Collected Poems of Frank O'Hara*. Edited by Donald Allen. New York: Knopf, 1971.

———. *Jackson Pollock*. New York: Braziller, 1959.

———. "Lament and Chastisement: A Travelogue of War and Personality." In *Early Writing*, edited by Donald Allen. Bolinas, Calif.: Grey Fox, 1977.

———. *Lunch Poems*. San Francisco: City Lights, 1964.

———. *Standing Still and Walking in New York*. Bolinas, Calif.: Grey Fox, 1975.

Oppen, George. *Collected Poems*. New York: New Directions, 1975.

———. Interview by L. S. Dembo. 1969. Reprinted in *The Contemporary Writer: Interviews with Sixteen Novelists and Poets*, edited by L. S. Dembo and Cyrena N. Pondrom. Madison: University of Wisconsin Press, 1972.

———. "The Mind's Own Place." *Kulchur* 10 (Summer 1963): 2–8.

———. *The Selected Letters of George Oppen*. Edited by Rachel Blau DuPlessis. Durham, N.C.: Duke University Press, 1990.

———. "Statement on Poetics." *Sagetrieb* 3 (Winter 1984): 25–27.

———. "Three Poets." Review of *Kaddish and Other Poems, 1958–1960*, by Allen Ginsberg; *Maximus from Dogtown*, by Charles Olson; *The Distances*, by Charles Olson; and *Dark Brown*, by Michael McClure. *Poetry* 100 (August 1962): 329–33.

Oppen, Mary. *Meaning a Life: An Autobiography*. Santa Barbara, Calif.: Black Sparrow, 1978.

Ostriker, Alicia. "In Mind: The Divided Self in Women's Poetry." In *Poetics: Essays on the Art of Poetry*, edited by Paul Mariani and George Murphy. Ocean Bluff, Mass: Tendril, 1984.

Perloff, Marjorie. *Frank O'Hara: Poet Among the Painters*. Austin: University of Texas Press, 1979.

———. "The Man Who Loved Women: The Medical Fictions of William Carlos Williams." *Georgia Review* 34 (1980): 840–53.

———. *The Poetics of Indeterminacy: Rimbaud to Cage*. Princeton: Princeton University Press, 1981.

———. "The Shape of the Lines: Oppen and the Metric of Difference." In *George George Oppen: Man and Poet*, edited by Burton Hatlen. Orono, Maine: National Poetry Foundation, 1981.

———. "The Shipwreck of the Singular: George Oppen's 'Of Being Numerous.'" In *George Oppen: Man and Poet*, edited by Burton Hatlen. Orono, Maine: National Poetry Foundation, 1981.

Pope, Deborah. *A Separate Vision: Isolation in Contemporary Women's Poetry*. Baton Rouge: Louisiana State University Press, 1984.

Pound, Ezra. *Literary Essays of Ezra Pound*. Edited by T. S. Eliot. 1935. Reprint, New York: New Directions, 1968.

Reising, Russell. *The Unusable Past: Theory and the Study of American Literature*. New York: Methuen, 1986.

Rexroth, Kenneth. "The New Poetry." In *Assays*. New York: New Directions, 1961.

Riddell, Joseph N. *The Inverted Bell: Modernism and the Counterpoetics of William Carlos Williams*. Baton Rouge: Louisiana State University Press, 1974.

Robbins, Bruce. "Modernism and Professionalism: The Case of William Carlos Williams." *Swiss Papers in English Language and Literature* 2 (1985): 191–205.

Rodden, John. *The Politics of Literary Reputation: The Making and Claiming of "St. George" Orwell*. New York: Oxford University Press, 1989.

Rosenberg, Harold. *The Anxious Object: Art Today and its Audience*. New York: Horizon Press, 1964.

Rosenfeld, Paul. *Port of New York*. 1924. Reprint, Urbana: University of Illinois Press, 1966.

Ross, Andrew. "The New Sentence and the Commodity Form: Recent American Writing." In *Marxism and the Interpretation of Culture*, edited by Cary Nelson and Lawrence Grossberg. Urbana: University of Illinois Press, 1988.

———, ed. *Universal Abandon?: The Politics of Postmodernism*. Minneapolis: University of Minnesota Press, 1988.

Rothenberg, Jerome. "Pre-face" to *Revolution of the Word: A New Gathering of American Avant-Garde Poetry, 1914–1945*, edited by Jerome Rothenberg. New York: Seabury, 1974.

Said, Edward W. *The World, the Text, and the Critic*. Cambridge: Harvard University Press, 1983.

Sakeilliou-Schultz, Linda. *Denise Levertov: An Annotated Primary and Secondary Bibliography*. New York: Garland, 1988.

Sayre, Henry. *The Visual Text of William Carlos Williams*. Urbana: University of Illinois Press, 1983.

Schmidt, Peter. *William Carlos Williams, The Arts, and Literary Tradition*. Baton Rouge: Louisiana State University Press, 1988.

Silliman, Ron. "Canons and Institutions: New Hope for the Disappeared." In *The Politics of Poetic Form*, edited by Charles Bernstein. New York: Roof, 1990.

———. "Language, Realism, Poetry." Introduction to *In the American Tree*, edited by Ron Silliman. Orono, Maine: National Poetry Foundation, 1986.

———. "Third Phase Objectivism." *Paideuma* 10 (Spring 1981): 85–89.

Simmel, Georg. "The Metropolis and Mental Life." In *The Sociology of Georg Simmel*. Translated and edited by Kurt H. Woolf. Glencoe, Ill.: The Free Press, 1950.

Smith, Lorrie. "Songs of Experience: Denise Levertov's Political Poetry." *Contemporary Literature* 27 (1986): 213–32.

Sollors, Werner. *Beyond Ethnicity: Consent and Descent in American Culture*. New York: Oxford University Press, 1986.

Sorrentino, Gilbert. "*Neon, Kulchur*, etc." In *The Little Magazine in America: A Modern Documentary History*, edited by Elliott Anderson and Mary Kinzie. Yonkers, N.Y.: Pushcart, 1978.

Spanos, William. "The De-struction of Form in Postmodern American Poetry: The Examples of Charles Olson and Robert Creeley." *Amerikastudien* 25 (1980): 375–404.

Stein, Gertrude. *Picasso: The Complete Writings*. Edited by Edward Burns. Boston: Beacon, 1985.

Surman, Diana. "Inside and Outside in the Poetry of Denise Levertov." *Critical Quarterly* 22 (1980): 57–70.

Tallman, Warren. Preface to *The Poetics of the New American Poetry*, edited by Donald Allen and Warren Tallman. New York: Grove, 1973.

Tapscott, Stephen. *American Beauty: William Carlos Williams and the Modernist Whitman*. New York: Columbia University Press, 1984.

Tashjian, Dickran. *Skyscraper Primitives: Dada and the American Avant-Garde, 1910–1925*. Middletown, Conn.: Wesleyan University Press, 1975.

———. *William Carlos Williams and the American Scene*. New York: Whitney Museum of American Art; Berkeley: University of California Press, 1978.

Terdiman, Richard. *Discourse/Counter-Discourse: The Theory and Practice of Symbolic Resistance in Nineteenth-Century France*. Ithaca: Cornell University Press, 1985.

Terrell, Carroll F., ed. *William Carlos Williams: Man and Poet*. Orono, Maine: National Poetry Foundation, 1983.

Thirlwall, John C. "William Carlos Williams' 'Paterson.'" *New Directions 17*. New York: New Directions, 1961.

Thomas, Brook. "The New Historicism and other Old-fashioned Topics." In *The New Historicism*, edited by H. Aram Vesser. New York: Routledge, 1989.

Tomlinson, Charles. Introduction to *William Carlos Williams: Selected Poems*, edited by Charles Tomlinson. New York: New Directions, 1985.

Uno, Hiroko. "Two Emily Dickinsons." *William Carlos Williams Review* 5 (1979): 220–22.

Vendler, Helen. *Part of Nature, Part of Us: Modern American Poets*. Cambridge: Harvard University Press, 1980.

von Hallberg, Robert. *American Poetry and Culture, 1945–1980*. Cambridge: Harvard University Press, 1985.

———. "The Politics of Description: William Carlos Williams in the Thirties." *ELH* 45 (1978): 131–51.

Wagner, Linda Welshimer. *Denise Levertov*. Boston: Twayne, 1967.

———. "William Carlos Williams." In *Sixteen Modern American Authors,* vol. 2, *A Survey of Research and Criticism*, edited by Jackson R. Bryer. Durham, N.C.: Duke University Press, 1990.

Weaver, Mike. *William Carlos Williams: The American Background*. Cambridge: Cambridge University Press, 1971.

Whitaker, Thomas R. *William Carlos Williams*. Boston: Twayne, 1968.

Williams, William Carlos. "America, Whitman, and the Art of Poetry." 1917. Reprinted in *William Carlos Review* 13.1 (1987): 1–4.

———. *The Autobiography of William Carlos Williams*. 1951. Reprint, New York: New Directions, 1967.

———. *The Collected Poems of William Carlos Williams*. Vol. 1, *1909–1939*. Edited by A. Walton Litz and Christopher MacGowan. New York: New Directions, 1986.

———. *The Collected Poems of William Carlos Williams*. Vol. 2, *1938–1962*. Edited by Christopher MacGowan. New York: New Directions, 1988.

———. *The Embodiment of Knowledge*. Edited by Ron Loewinsohn. New York: New Directions, 1974.

———. *Imaginations*. Containing *Kora in Hell*, 1920; *Spring and All*, 1923; *The Great American Novel*, 1923; *The Descent of Winter*, 1928; *A Novelette and Other Prose*, 1932. Edited by Webster Schott. New York: New Directions, 1970.

———. *In the American Grain*. 1925. Reprint, New York: New Directions, 1956.

———. *I Wanted to Write a Poem: The Autobiography of the Works of a Poet*. Reported and edited by Edith Heal. New York: New Directions, 1958.

————. *Make Light of It: Collected Stories*. New York: Random House, 1950.

————. "The New Poetical Economy." 1934. Reprinted in *George Oppen: Man and Poet*, edited by Burton Hatlen. Orono, Maine: National Poetry Foundation, 1981.

————. *Selected Essays of William Carlos Williams*. New York: Random House, 1954.

————. *The Selected Letters of William Carlos Williams*. Edited by John C. Thirlwall. New York: McDowell, Oblensky, 1957.

Williams, William Carlos, and James Laughlin. *Selected Letters*. Edited by Hugh Witemeyer. New York: Norton, 1989.

Zukofsky, Louis. "American Poetry, 1920–1930." 1930. Reprinted in *Prepositions: The Collected Critical Essays of Louis Zukofsky*. Expanded ed. Berkeley: University of California Press, 1981.

————. "Program: 'Objectivists' 1931." *Poetry* 38 (February 1931): 268–72.

Index

Allen, Donald M., 13, 119, 146n. 2, 147
n. 3; *The New American Poetry*, 13,
146n. 2, 147n. 3, 156n. 11
Altieri, Charles, 115, 157n. 17, 158n. 7
Antin, David, 146n. 2
Apollinaire, Guillaume, 102, 108
Ashbery, John, 149n. 14
Auden, W. H., 108
Avant-gardism, 15–16; American
compared to European, 15, 17–18.
See also O'Hara, Frank; Williams,
William Carlos

Baker, Peter, 158n. 5
Bakhtin, M. M., 16
Baldwin, Neil, 155n. 6
Barthes, Roland, 114
Bate, Walter Jackson, 75
Baudelaire, Charles, 102
Behan, Brendan, 116
Benjamin, Walter, 17
Bernstein, Charles, 13
Bernstein, Michael André, 160n. 6
Berry, Eleanor, 160n. 4
Bertens, Hans, 150n. 14
Black Mountain poetics, 79
Blasing, Mutlu Konuk, 151n. 24, 158n. 5
Bloom, Harold, 75–76, 122, 148n. 6
Bogan, Louise, 146n. 2
Boone, Bruce, 158n. 4
Boyle, Kay, 41
Brecht, Bertolt, 17
Breslin, James E. B., 19, 58, 78–79, 148
n. 6, 154nn. 30 and 1, 156nn. 11 and
12, 158n. 5
Breslin, Paul, 150–51n. 24, 157n. 17

Bronk, William, 137
Brooks, Van Wyk, 43, 45; *America's
Coming of Age*, 43
Brown, Edmund, 31
Burger, Peter, 17

Canon formation, 13–16, 23–24, 29–30,
147n. 3, 149n. 8
Clifford, James, 69–70
Coles, Robert, 154n. 1
Conrad, Bryce, 43–44
Contact, 18
Corso, Gregory: "Bomb," 109
Costello, Bonnie, 156–57n. 17
Creeley, Robert, 18–19, 20–21, 24, 74, 79
Culler, Jonathan, 35
Cultural memory, 13–16

Davis, Miles, 119
Degnan, June Oppen, 160n.3
Dickinson, Emily, 41–42, 153n. 20
Dijkstra, Bram, 154n. 6
Driscoll, Kerry, 153n. 17, 157n. 17
Duchamp, Marcel, 17, 18
Duncan, Robert, 21
DuPlessis, Rachel Blau, 80–81, 136,
156n. 17, 160n. 13

Eliot, T. S., 18, 20, 23, 29–30, 43, 75, 112,
137; "Tradition and the Individual
Talent," 111; "The Waste Land," 128.
See also Williams, William Carlos
Ernst, Max, 108

Fellini, Federico, 120
Ferlinghetti, Lawrence, 156n. 9

171

Pound, Ezra, 13, 27–28, 43, 55, 58, 75, 79, 125, 137, 154 n. 2; "In a Station of the Metro," 55. *See also* Levertov, Denise; Oppen, George

Rasles, Sebastien, 44–48; *Lettres édifiantes*, 44
Reising, Russell, 152 n. 5
Reverdy, Pierre, 102
Rexroth, Kenneth, 146 n. 2
Rich, Adrienne, 80–81
Riddell, Joseph: *The Inverted Bell*, 26
Rilke, Rainer Maria, 85–86
Rimbaud, Arthur, 108, 116
Robbins, Bruce, 149 n. 11
Rodden, John, 14–15
Rosenberg, Harold, 121–22
Rosenfeld, Paul: *Port of New York*, 27–28
Ross, Andrew, 150 n. 24
Rothenberg, Jerome, 146 n. 2
Rukeyser, Muriel, 80–81

Said, Edward W., 29–30
Sakeilliou-Schultz, Linda, 156 n. 11
Sandburg, Carl, 136–37
Sayre, Henry, 150 n. 24, 154–55 n. 6
Schmidt, Peter, 14, 56–57, 153 n. 14
Sewall, Richard: *Life of Emily Dickinson*, 153 n. 20
Shakespeare, William: *As You Like It*, 34
Silliman, Ron, 20, 125, 149 n. 8, 156 n. 11; *In the American Tree*, 20
Simmel, Georg, 123
Smith, Lorrie, 156–57 n. 17
Sorrentino, Gilbert, 19, 21
Stein, Gertrude, 107–8
Stevens, Wallace, 55–56, 109
Surman, Diana, 156 n. 12

Tallman, Warren, 147 n. 3
Tapscott, Stephen, 153 n. 13
Tashjian, Dickran, 30, 154–55 n. 6
Terdiman, Richard, 16
Thirlwall, John C., 153 n. 17
Toklas, Alice B., 108
Tomlinson, Charles, 18
Trilling, Lionel, 119
Twain, Mark, 34

Vendler, Helen, 102
Verlaine, Paul, 116
von Hallberg, Robert, 114, 139

Wagner, Linda Welshimer, 156 n. 12
Wagner-Martin, Linda, 148 n. 6
Wakoski, Diane, 18–19
Warhol, Andy, 109–10
Wellcome, Emily Dickinson, 37, 38–42
Whitman, Walt, 44, 102. Works: "Crossing Brooklyn Ferry," 33, 35; *Leaves of Grass*, 32, 55; "Passage to India," 35. *See also* Williams, William Carlos
Williams, William Carlos: on the "American idiom," 20–24; articulation as trope in, 49–54; avant-garde practice of, 16–18, 61–62; descent as trope in, 16, 26; and Eliot, 62–63, 154 n. 26.; and ethnic identity, 25–32; influence on postwar poetry, 18–21, 74–75, 125, 148 n. 6; literary reputation of, 13–15, 19; and localism, 18, 33; and Marxism, 17, 139; medical practice of, 49–52, 154 n. 1; and objectivism, 76, 79, 129–30; and puritanism, 16, 44–48; and translation, 49; and Whitman, 24, 31–38, 55. *See also* Levertov, Denise; O'Hara, Frank; Oppen, George. Works: *Al Que Quire!*, 30–32, 56; "America, Whitman and the Art of Poetry" (essay), 24, 32–33; "The American Background" (essay), 18, 41; "Apology," 56; "At the Ball Game" (67); *The Autobiography of William Carlos Williams*, 41, 49–52, 102–4, 129, 153 n. 19; "The Avenue of Poplars," 155 n. 11; "The Banner Bearer," 84–86; "Death the Barber," 66; "Dedication for a Plot of Ground," 38–42; *Della Primavera Trasportata al Morale*, 33; *The Descent of Winter*, 33, 100; *The Embodiment of Knowledge*, 52–54; "The Farmer," 65; "Flight to the City," 155 n. 11; "Foreign," 56; "Gulls," 56; "Impromptu: The Suckers," 56; *In the American Grain*,